The
Story
Behind
the *Smile*

Lynn McMahon

Globe
Pequot

Blue Ridge Summit, PA

Globe Pequot

An imprint of Globe Pequot, the trade division of
The Rowman & Littlefield Publishing Group, Inc.
4501 Forbes Blvd., Ste. 200
Lanham, MD 20706
www.rowman.com

Distributed by NATIONAL BOOK NETWORK

British Library Cataloguing in Publication Information available

Library of Congress Control Number: 2022945177

978-1-4930-7426-6 (paper)
978-1-4930-7427-3 (electronic)

♾™The paper used in this publication meets the minimum requirements of American National Standard for Information Sciences—Permanence of Paper for Printed Library Materials, ANSI/NISO Z39.48-1992.

Dedication

To Larry Hatch who invited me into the Eat'n Park family and gave me the chance of a lifetime to work with thousands of dedicated team members who helped to evolve Eat'n Park Hospitality Group into what it is today.

— Jim Broadhurst

A portion of the proceeds from the sale of
The Story Behind the Smile will benefit
UPMC Children's Hospital of Pittsburgh through
Eat'n Park Hospitality Group's Caring for Kids Campaign.

Designed by MJ Creative Team
Original cover concept: Scot Wallace Design
Photography: Eat'n Park Hospitality Group Archives, John Altdorfer (page 161),
Brooks Broadhurst, Bill Moore, Nicholas Michalenko, Adam Stephenson,
Pittsburgh Post-Gazette (page 133)

Contents

Preface

Prologue: Larry Hatch and Jim Broadhurst:
Contrasts and Complements

Chapter 1: The Early Years: Embracing Innovation   1

Chapter 2: The Growth Years: A New Vision   17

Chapter 3: Another Evolution: People, Places,
and Perspectives   31

Chapter 4: A Traveling Show of Appreciation   49

Chapter 5: Parkhurst: Diversifying for the Future   55

Chapter 6: Giving Birth to a Parent Company:
Eat'n Park Hospitality Group   85

Chapter 7: An Appetite for Pleasing Palates   91

Chapter 8: A Community of Caring   113

Chapter 9: Smiley: From Sweet Cookie to Superstar Icon 127

Chapter 10: Innovation and Compassion:
The North Star for Navigating a Pandemic   137

Chapter 11: Eat'n Park Hospitality Group Culture:
A Family of 10,000   149

Epilogue   162

Acknowledgements   164

About the Author   165

Bibliography   166

Preface

Jim Broadhurst handed me a box of Smiley Cookies. It was the early 1990s, and Jim was the chair of the Board of Trustees of Children's Hospital of Pittsburgh (now UPMC Children's Hospital of Pittsburgh). I was the hospital's vice president of public relations and had written remarks for Jim to deliver at the opening of a new service area at the hospital. The cookies were Jim's way of thanking me for the effort. It made me smile.

What began as writing for hospital-related activities expanded into writing for the Eat'n Park Restaurants' newsletter and some of Jim's business communications, after we both had moved on from our association with the hospital. In 2000, Jim invited me to meet over lunch where I learned that he wanted me to help him write remarks for a commencement address he was to deliver at Robert Morris University. It felt like a monumental task.

We worked closely on that speech, and I began to know Jim as more than the head of a corporation, more than a hospital leader. I learned to better understand his perspective on life, the importance of his family, his philosophy about business, and his commitment to serving others. I learned about his authenticity. I learned about his humbleness.

As my work with Jim continued over the years, I had the opportunity to meet his wife, Suzy, who I quickly discovered matched Jim's attributes perfectly. Suzy's compassion and understanding of the human spirit were the touchstones for her leadership in developing and implementing the company's programs to support the community.

Eventually, I met "the boys." Today, it probably seems odd that I refer to Jeff, Brooks, and Mark as boys, but when I met them, they were, indeed, boys. It was later that they, too, became leaders in the community and in business.

In 2013, the Broadhurst family – 12 people at the time – traveled to Africa for a safari to interact with the indigenous people, learn about their lifestyle, and see the array of native animals. When they returned, Jim asked me to help him write a book about an amazing family vacation. He wanted the book to capture for posterity how the Broadhursts learned about the closeness of family against a backdrop of a distant continent.

Writing the safari book took my relationship with the Broadhurst family to a deeper level. They welcomed me into their home so that I could talk with their daughters-in-law Sheryl and Jen (Amy hadn't yet entered the scene). Sheryl and Jen were warm, welcoming, and genuine – just like every other member of the family. I remember wondering how it was possible that in-laws could have the same qualities as those born into the family.

During that visit, I also spent time with Jim and Suzy's grandchildren to hear their anecdotes from the safari. Kyle and Ryan, and Cora, Jack, and Charlie shared stories with me about their adventures – stories they will undoubtedly one day share with their younger cousin, Lilly.

As a writer and public relations practitioner, I enjoy the privilege of having Eat'n Park Hospitality Group as a long-time client. The Hospitality Group invites their business partners (referred to as "vendors" by many companies) to attend a biennial general managers' conference. The partners pay their own way and learn details about the growth, opportunities, and challenges of the Hospitality Group.

At the 2014 general managers' conference at The Greenbrier, Jim told me that he thought the time would soon be right for a book about the history of Eat'n Park, and he wanted to talk with me about writing it. It was a moment that remains etched in my memory.

It took a couple of years for the time to be right. What followed was a series of discussions among Jim, Suzy, and me about how the book might take shape. We decided the best way to tell the story of a single restaurant developing into a hospitality group would be through the stories of the people who made it happen.

Once we had the vision defined, the interviewing began in 2018. I met with team members in restaurants and at client sites, compiling memory after memory. Jim, Suzy, Kathy James (Jim's executive assistant), and I met frequently – sometimes at the Broadhurst home, sometimes during retreats and conferences, most often at the company's headquarters. The pieces were starting to come together. Until April 2020.

The COVID-19 pandemic had placed the hospitality industry squarely in its focus, and there was nothing but uncertainty about what the ramifications would be. So, for one year, the elements of the book were digitally tucked away.

The decline of the pandemic enabled us to resume our work on the book in April 2021, and we did so with renewed energy and enthusiasm. Meetings with Jim, Suzy, and Kathy were literally and figuratively turning pages in a photo album. There were so many memories of team members, stories about the early days and the rudimentary way things were done, questions about "Whatever happened to…", and stories about current team members and the value they add to the company. Meetings, phone calls, and shared meals resulted in sentimental memories, excitement about the future, and additional material for the book. One of my unexpected pleasures was witnessing the playfulness between Suzy and Jim and how much they enjoyed poking a little fun at each other – and themselves – throughout a project that consumed so much of their time and energy.

Over the course of three years, I interviewed more than 60 people, each of whom was eager to relay stories. I talked with Bill Moore, the grandson of the founder of Eat'n Park, and he provided valuable information about Larry Hatch, Bob and Claire Moore, and the development of the company. I talked with people who began their careers in an early era, including carhops Katie Freyer and Nancy Mathews; people who are current-day inspirations, including Suzie Lachut with the Parkhurst Dining Division; Mercy Senchur with the Restaurant Division; and Dan Wilson and Rich Liebscher with Eat'n Park Hospitality Group; and long-time team members who are the heart and soul of the company, including Kathy James, Carol Kijanka, and Patty Shell.

What became evident through meeting these individuals is the pride they have in being a part of the Eat'n Park Hospitality Group family. For them, it's never simply a job; it's a privilege.

As you read *The Story Behind the Smile*, I hope that you will learn how the Broadhursts built upon the foundation of Larry Hatch, the founder of Eat'n Park, to establish a defined culture of the company – a culture that team members today embrace and continue to infuse throughout every Eat'n Park Hospitality Group brand. And I also hope that for you, reading the stories that follow will help to create a smile.

Larry Hatch and Jim Broadhurst
Contrasts and Complements

Claire "Larry" Hatch was a frequent customer of Isaly's, a chain of dairy stores throughout Ohio, owned by the Isaly family. Lore has it that, as a customer, Hatch provided the owners with some unsolicited advice about streamlining processes and increasing profits. Soon, Hatch was an Isaly's employee. The year was 1931.

Claire "Larry" Hatch

Hatch was sent to Pittsburgh to oversee six Isaly's stores. In 1948, on a business trip to Cincinnati, Hatch discovered Frisch's, a drive-in restaurant that served a hamburger called Big Boy®.

Within a year, Hatch developed a concept he called Eat'n Park – a drive-in restaurant with limited indoor seating – and he became a Big Boy franchisee. After opening a few Eat'n Park locations, Hatch offered the concept to the Isaly family, but they were committed to staying the course as dairy specialists with neighborhood stores.

With 15 Eat'n Park locations in operation, Larry Hatch departed Isaly's in 1960 to focus on Eat'n Park. He went on to continue to expand and evolve the restaurant concept for more than 10 years with the help of Bill Peters.

One hundred miles north of Pittsburgh, Titusville was home to the Broadhurst family: Elmore (whose height earned him the nickname "Stretch") and Clara, and their four children, Ann, Jim, Susan, and Beth. It was a close family, attending the local Episcopal church every Sunday where the children's grandfather was the preacher.

Young Jimmy Broadhurst

Little Jimmy Broadhurst was a happy kid who enjoyed being outdoors, playing ball, riding his bike, and snacking on a sugar cookie on his way home from school. While Jimmy was enjoying his family and friends, he didn't know that back in Pittsburgh, something was taking shape that would change his life, the life of his future family, and generations to follow: On Sunday, June 5, 1949, at 2:00 in the afternoon, Eat'n Park, "Pittsburgh's First Modern Eat-in-Your-Car Food Service," was opening at 2209 Saw Mill Run Boulevard.

In the early 1970s, Larry Hatch met a young banker named Jim Broadhurst. He quickly grew to appreciate Jim's business savvy and principled approach to business. Within a couple of years, Jim was onboard at Eat'n Park, complementing Larry's history with his own vision for the future.

In 1984, Jim and his wife, Suzy, assumed ownership of Eat'n Park Restaurants, building upon the foundation of his predecessor and adding greater emphasis on training and developing the employee team, strengthening the company's financial performance, and enhancing the company's culture. His upbringing in the industrial town of Titusville taught Jim the value of hard work and the importance of family – traits that he wove into his leadership of the company.

The Story Behind the Smile is the history of how a singular roadside restaurant grew from Big Boy hamburgers and carhops into a multi-dimensional hospitality group.

1

The Early Years
Embracing Innovation

Innovation has been at the crux of Eat'n Park Restaurants since its founding in 1949. To understand its significance requires stepping back in history to the years prior to the opening of the first restaurant. Surprisingly, Eat'n Park's roots are intertwined with another brand well recognized in the Pittsburgh area – Isaly's.

Claire "Larry" Hatch was born in Auburn, New York, and moved to Welland, Canada, where his father accepted a job in a steel mill during World War I. He played hockey, tennis, baseball, and basketball. His daughter Claire Moore relayed, "He didn't like basketball, but living in a small town and being 6'3", he didn't have much choice!"

How Larry Hatch began with Isaly's depends on your perspective.

According to Larry's daughter Claire, after playing for a minor league Canadian baseball team, Larry moved to West Virginia and worked for Scott's 5 & 10. When the store transferred him to Youngstown, he frequently lunched at Isaly's, a family-owned, neighborhood dairy store. "That's where he built a relationship with Charly Isaly," Claire explained.

Isaly's executives, left to right: Forbes, Sayre, Isaly, Hatch, and McClain

"Knowing that my father wanted to move to Pittsburgh, Charly sent a note to his brother Sam, the manager of Isaly's Youngstown stores, and told him to hire him. And if they didn't have a place for him in Pittsburgh, Charly told his brother to find a place in Ohio. They didn't want anyone else to hire him."

Isaly's history documents Larry Hatch's beginnings with the company a little differently. According to the book *Klondikes, Chipped Ham, & Skyscraper Cones: The Story of Isaly's* by Brian Butko, during Hatch's frequent visits to a neighborhood Isaly's, he observed a continuing stream of salesmen calling on the store manager. He thought that the Isaly's franchises would benefit from a buying cooperative. It would cut back on the interruptions created by a parade of uninvited salesmen trying to win business for their line of products. After running the buying-cooperative idea by managers at several Isaly's stores, a self-assured Hatch brought it to the attention of Sam Isaly. After hearing Hatch's idea, Sam offered him a job.

Both Larry's daughter and Isaly's history agree that a few weeks after starting with the company, Sam sent Larry east to manage the family's six struggling stores in Pittsburgh. Hatch was widely regarded as blunt, but regardless of – or because of – his style, he put the Pittsburgh stores back in the black.

It was the spring of 1931, and regardless of the exact details of Larry Hatch's early career with Isaly's, no one could have predicted his impact on either Isaly's or on a still-to-be-envisioned family restaurant.

While he was working in Pittsburgh, Larry received a call from a friend telling him about a Cincinnati restaurant he had just discovered that had a menu item called Frisch's Big Boy®. It was a drive-in restaurant operation and, according to Larry's friend, their sales were "unbelievable."

Larry made the trip to Cincinnati and immediately was intrigued by Frisch's drive-in restaurant concept. It was the late 1940s, World War II had ended, and automobiles were becoming more commonplace on American streets. Looking at the drive-in restaurant and how it was changing dining patterns, Larry could see that the car industry would have a huge effect on American lifestyles.

Like his friend, Larry also was intrigued by Big Boy. Two hamburgers were sandwiched between three bun slices with shredded lettuce, cheese, pickles, and a sauce. The Big Boy image was a chubby young boy wearing red-and-white checkerboard overalls, carrying a tray with the special hamburger. As Hatch observed the drive-in restaurant activity, he could see the item clearly was a big seller for Frisch's.

Larry returned to Pittsburgh. Thinking about that drive-in restaurant, his mind was running as fast as a Packard Clipper. He would introduce a drive-in restaurant to his adopted hometown of Pittsburgh. And he wanted that Big Boy. Frisch's had the copyright on the Big Boy name in Ohio, so Hatch filed for and received a copyright for the name in southwest Pennsylvania.

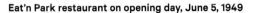

Fulfilling a Vision

Taking out a second mortgage on the home he shared with his wife, Gladys, Larry was able to obtain the $75,000 necessary to buy a parcel on Saw Mill Run Boulevard/Route 51 in the South Hills of Pittsburgh. On Sunday, June 5, 1949, at 2:00 in the afternoon, Larry Hatch – with absolutely no restaurant experience – opened the first Eat'n Park restaurant. It was the drive-in restaurant he dreamed of – and the first in Pittsburgh – with 10 outdoor stalls, 13 indoor seats, and 10 carhops.

The response on the opening Sunday afternoon was so overwhelming, traffic backed onto busy Route 51 as cars waited for a parking spot. Hatch had planned for all opening-day diners to receive a free ice cream sundae. To keep the occupants of the waiting cars happy, the waitresses delivered them to ease their wait. The precedent was set: do your best to keep the customer happy.

Eat'n Park restaurant on opening day, June 5, 1949

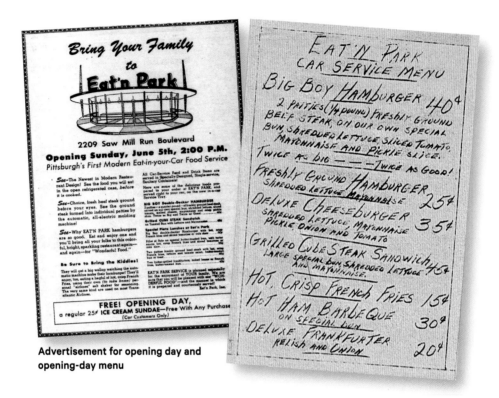

Advertisement for opening day and opening-day menu

Despite the team's efforts, the growing crowd forced Larry to temporarily close the restaurant while he developed a simpler menu. When the restaurant re-opened the next day, the condensed menu enabled faster prep and cooking, and faster delivery to hungry customers.

To help with the opening, several Isaly's employees and members of the Hatch family volunteered their time, even though none of them had ever worked in a restaurant. Each night when the restaurant closed, one of the volunteers, Neff Jenkins, would take the day's receipts back to Larry and Gladys's house where he was staying. He put the cash under his bed, waiting for the bank to open the next day. It was a simpler time.

Another volunteer, Bill Peters, was one of the managers of a Pittsburgh Isaly's store. Since Larry was working full time at Isaly's, he needed a trusted friend to manage the fledgling Eat'n Park restaurant. Bill was the solution. In 1950-51, Larry persuaded Bill to give up his job with Isaly's to become president of Eat'n Park Restaurants. His help in getting the first restaurants up and running was invaluable to Larry. Bill was president for more than 20 years, until declining health forced him to retire in 1973.

Some people were puzzled by the name of the new restaurant, thinking the more appropriate name was Park & Eat. Afterall, that describes the experience more accurately. In the 1940s, Park & Eat was a generic term used as directional signage for a number of restaurants, so Larry Hatch and Bill Peters doubted the likelihood of having a trademark of the words. Legend has it that, with a nod to the ubiquity of Park and Eat signs, they quickly decided to flip the order of the words to Eat'n Park and developed an explanatory slogan: "Come as you are – Eat in your car."

Next Steps

Larry continued in his role with Isaly's while further developing his restaurant concept. With the success of his first restaurant, he easily attracted other investors. Among the early investors were Reed Agnew, an architect; Harold Kirk, an accountant; and P.J. Harmon, owner of Harmon Lumber. After a few years, Hatch was able to buy back the stock Harmon and Kirk owned. Agnew, however, required a creative business approach. Hatch had financed an office in Mt. Lebanon, and Agnew designed the building. When Agnew grew unhappy with the lack of dividends from the restaurant, Hatch traded the building for Agnew's stock.

The second Eat'n Park restaurant, located in Avalon, opened four months after the first. When he had five restaurants open, Larry went back to Sam Isaly to offer them to Isaly's. But Isaly wasn't interested. He wanted to keep his stores focused on their role as neighborhood dairy stores; he believed that was the future.

As Eat'n Park Restaurants grew, Larry was demanding of his staff. "He wanted things done right away or sooner," remembered Bob Moore. "He saw the big picture; he didn't worry about the details." Bob Moore had an interesting perspective: he joined Eat'n Park as a grill man in July 1951, the day after he returned from his honeymoon with his bride, Claire Hatch, Larry's daughter.

By 1960, Larry Hatch decided the time was right for him to leave Isaly's and devote his energy exclusively to Eat'n Park. But he remained in the background. Employees recognized Bill Peters as president and, in fact, few even knew Larry Hatch.

The History of Big Boy

In the late 1930s in Glendale, California, Bob Wian sold his 1933 DeSoto Roadster for $350 and used the funds to purchase a 10-seat hamburger chain. He named it Bob's Pantry. Bob, who in high school was voted "Least Likely to Succeed," had a friend visit the restaurant and ask for something different to eat. As a joke, Bob cut a sesame-seed bun into three horizontal slices, placed two hamburger patties between them, and finished the sandwich with lettuce, cheese, and his special pickle relish. "The whole idea just took off," Bob said of his Big Boy creation.

Bob's Pantry: birthplace of the Big Boy Burger

An equally casual event created the image long associated with that sandwich. The double-decker burger was a favorite of a young customer in Bob's Pantry – a chubby 6-year-old boy in droopy overalls. Another frequent customer – an animator – used a napkin as his canvas and sketched the now-famous drawing that was the start of the image that became the symbol of Big Boy.

In southwestern Pennsylvania, Larry succeeded in securing the copyright to the Big Boy name. His visit to Frisch's in Cincinnati inspired both car service and the addition of Big Boy sandwiches to the menu in the new Eat'n Park restaurants.

In late 1949, Bob Wian visited Larry and Bill Peters to discuss the copyright. He demonstrated that he had originated the Big Boy sandwich and had a national copyright on the name and the symbol. Bob realized, however, that it would be virtually impossible to enforce the copyright since – in addition to Eat'n Park and Frisch's – there were many restaurants using the Big Boy name, including Shoney's (in the south), Azar's (Indiana), Elias Brothers (Michigan), Abdows (New England), Elby's (West Virginia), and Manner's (Ohio).

Bob developed a plan to set up a franchise of the name and the sandwich with the original operators. The symbol of Big Boy had slight variations from market to market, but he always ended up dressed in checkered pants. There also were different sauces. For example, in the west at Bob's Big Boy restaurants, they used a red sauce, similar to Thousand Island dressing. Other restaurants, including Frisch's and Eat'n Park, used a white sauce, similar to tartar sauce. The compromise was to have a western sauce and an eastern sauce.

Satisfied with the compromise, Bill Peters and Bob Wian signed an agreement on the use of the name Big Boy and the composition of the sandwich. The agreement covered a period of 25 years, from 1949 to 1974, and enabled Bob to claim a national presence, a claim necessary to obtain a federal trademark. The franchise cost was $1 a year. To fulfill Eat'n Park's financial obligation, Bill Peters sent Wian an old, wrinkled dollar bill each year.

In 1967, Bob Wian sold his chain of Bob's Big Boy Restaurants to Marriott Corporation, reportedly for $7 million, and transferred the ownership of the Big Boy copyright.

When Eat'n Park's Big Boy agreement ended in 1974, Jim Broadhurst was executive vice president and treasurer of the company and opted to not enter into a new agreement with Marriott. Presumably, the terms would have been considerably more than the $1 annual fee. "It was more like 2% of sales," Bob Moore remembered. "Jim Broadhurst came up with a very strong, 'No way.'" Eat'n Park dropped the Big Boy name and image, and in place of the Big Boy burger, the restaurant introduced the Superburger®. "We didn't miss a beat," Bob said.

In 1967, Bob Wian sold his chain of Bob's Big Boy Restaurants to Marriott Corporation, reportedly for $7 million and transferred the ownership of the Big Boy copyright.

Carhops: Driving into the Future

When Larry Hatch observed the carhop service at Frisch's restaurant in Cincinnati, he knew it was a rising wave. Cars were becoming more accessible and having a significant effect on the American way of life. Hatch reasoned that car service could become a new dimension in the restaurant business. Although car service is frequently associated with the 1950s, thanks to movies like "American Graffiti," it remained popular through the mid-1970s. Movies popularized images of carhops on roller skates; however, Eat'n Park carhops kept their feet securely on the ground.

Car service was more than a means of ordering a meal; it was a part of pop culture. In fact, in western Pennsylvania, Eat'n Park defined pop culture.

"Friday nights, the cars would just line around the edges of the parking lot, and the lights were on, and everybody was out talking," remembers Nancy Mathews, former carhop and current server at Eat'n Park's Whitehall restaurant. "It was really fun."

On some weekend nights, guests would visit multiple Eat'n Park locations. "They were driving around and going from Whitehall to South Park to Dormont to Banksville," Nancy remembers. "They would do that loop then come back to Whitehall."

"We told them to 'Come as you are, eat in your car,' and, boy, did they!" Bob Moore remembered. "Women with curlers, unshaven men, kids jumping up and down all over the car – our carhops put up with a lot."

A Family Affair

From the opening of the first Eat'n Park restaurant in 1949 until the mid-1970s, the role for women was clear: carhops. One carhop, Helen, inspired her young daughter, Katie Schanck (now Freyer) to follow in her footsteps.

"My mother started in August of 1968 as a carhop at Whitehall," Katie relates. "She had seven kids and was recently separated, and she needed a job. A neighbor worked there and said, 'Well, why don't you come up here, Helen?' So, she went up and worked there for 24 years."

In April 1970, Katie was ready for her first job, so she followed her mother to the Whitehall Eat'n Park, where she started working as a carhop. "It was the best job I ever had," Katie says. "I was 16 years old, all of my friends were there hanging out in the lot, and I was getting paid to be there."

As Eat'n Park began to phase out car service, carhops were given the opportunity to work in the dining room. When Katie moved inside, she and her mom rarely worked the same shift. But Katie never felt lonely because five of her six siblings also worked at the restaurant along with her mother's sister and five of her cousins.

Technology of the Time

The logistics of how car service operated was part science and part ingenuity. The carhop area at Eat'n Park restaurants was divided into sections with stalls. When cars parked in the lot, the guests turned on the car headlights to signal their arrival to the carhops.

Carhops would welcome guests and drop off a menu. Of course, the menu included the Big Boy hamburger, as well as ham barbeque, hot dogs, cold sandwiches, French fries, milk shakes, and sundaes.

After the guests ordered, the carhop gave them a number to place in their car and directed them to turn off their headlights. When the order was ready, the cook would call the carhop's number through a loudspeaker. Carhops delivered orders on trays that attached to car windows.

Each parking stall was numbered to make it easier for the carhop to find the correct car. But if the guest moved the car, it was then up to the carhop to track it down in the lot. When guests were finished with their meal, they turned on their headlights to signal the carhops that the tray was ready to be removed.

In the 1960s, technology evolved carhop service. Teletrays were added to each stall, along with a menu and an intercom. The guest pushed a button that would light up inside the restaurant. Whoever answered the call took the order and served it.

The Whitehall Eat'n Park had 48 stalls. "Nobody ever wanted to wait on #48 because that was all the way in the back of the lot," Katie Freyer remembers. "It was too far a walk, and it was usually some troublemaking kid that we were going to have to deal with."

Walking Cash Registers

Carhops were each given $10 at the beginning of their shift to use to make change. They wore a change maker and a double-pocket pouch attached to their belt. One pocket was for cash, the other for menus.

"I remember my dad teaching me how to make change when I was 16 years old," Nancy Mathews says. "We practiced at the kitchen table. He would say, 'OK, if I give you this much money, how much are you going to give me back?' We'd play out all these different scenarios so that I knew how to give change to people."

At the end of the carhop's shift, she turned in the money she collected for her checks and the original $10. Everything that remained was the carhop's to keep. "When a carhop turned in $100 in checks, we considered her an outstanding employee," Bob Moore remembered.

"A good day back then was probably $6 - $8 in tips," Katie Freyer laughs. "When you're 16, that's good!"

Meanwhile, one or two waitresses were stationed inside the restaurant to take care of the customers at the 13-seat counter. They also prepared milkshakes, sodas, and sundaes for car-service guests.

For Katie, the most difficult part of the job was cleaning the teletrays at the 10:00 a.m. start of a shift. The trays often had remnants of the previous night's dinners, and there was one condiment that was particularly difficult to clean.

"If it was winter, ketchup would be frozen on the trays," says Katie. "We actually used windshield washer fluid in water because it didn't freeze, so that's how we cleaned them in the morning."

"And then at the end of the night, you always had to go out and sweep the lot," adds Nancy. "No matter what. Rain, sleet, snow, because Big Boys were wrapped in cellophane with a little cardboard neck on them to keep them straight. People would eat the burger and throw the cellophane and cardboard out the window. So, we'd have to go out at night and sweep the lot," she says. "Oh, it could be really messy, but it got done every night."

Tough Love

"Car service was a challenge," remembers Dan Meharey who, at the peak of car service, was a restaurant manager. "Nobody was supposed to be out of their vehicles. But people were out, running around and talking, and that's the way it was. As a manager, you'd go out and say, 'OK guys, you need to get in your car,' and as you turned around, they'd be throwing French fries at you!

An Eat'n Park lot on a typical weekend evening at the height of carhop service

"On the weekends, we'd have lot cops. They were local police we paid that would just come, stand out in the parking lot, and make sure everybody was staying in their cars. But some lot cops weren't that great.

"I said to a lot cop, 'How about telling those guys to get in their cars?' He said, 'My job's only to stop fights.' I said, 'I don't care if they fight. They can kill each other for all I care. Get them in their cars!'"

A Changing Landscape

As Eat'n Park continued to expand, a new competitor –McDonald's® – entered the marketplace. Yellow arches were popping up everywhere.

Crucial decisions needed to be made regarding the future success of Eat'n Park. "I have no doubt in my mind that it was the walk-up McDonald's that spelled the end of car service," Bob Moore said. "They came in with faster service because they cooked ahead. They also had a cheaper menu, which they could afford because of such a low payroll, and customers did not tip. Eat'n Park had a big decision to make as the handwriting was on the wall."

When Jim Broadhurst joined the company in 1973, he and Larry Hatch identified three possible paths they could take with the young restaurant: 1) keep it the way it was; 2) change it to be

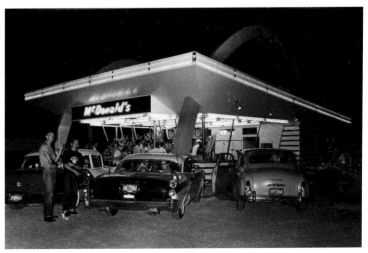

The arrival of McDonald's triggered an inflection point for Eat'n Park.

more like McDonald's; or 3) offer the consumer something completely different. Larry and Jim decided to take the most costly and riskiest path. They decided to offer the consumer something completely different by transforming drive-in restaurants into sit-down restaurants.

Helping with decision making was the economics of carhop service. "Friday nights were our busiest nights," explains Keith Lester, a retired district manager with Eat'n Park. "Back then, the parking lot was filled with cars of teens and college students drinking dollar sodas and taking up parking spaces. People couldn't spend money in the dining room because they couldn't find a place to park."

As the carhop service began to be phased out, the physical transformation of restaurants began. Additional seating was added, drive-in canopies were torn down, and electronic systems and new equipment were incorporated to adapt to a new menu. The carhops became waitresses. "The switchover from car service to an inside restaurant was a gradual one," Bob Moore said. "We would phase out car service in two or three restaurants at a time."

The final car service ended December 26, 1977, with the Aliquippa, Monongahela, Large, Library Road, and Whitehall Eat'n Park restaurants the last to make the change. "It was a little more emotional for me because my mother was a carhop and my sister was a carhop," remembers Keith Lester who, at the time, was a general manager at the Library Road restaurant on Route 88 near the entrance to South Park. "It's who we are; the name says it; how can we not have curbside service?" he remembers thinking.

Before Keith was an Eat'n Park team member, he was an Eat'n Park guest, and he remembers that guests embraced the change. "We used to come down right from the school, straight down to the Monongahela Eat'n Park," Keith says. "It was an assumption, the game was over, you went to Eat'n Park. And you tried to get there quick, because Eat'n Park put police officers at the door to control how many people went in and out, so that they didn't exceed the maximum seating. And if you weren't one of the first ones in, then you had to wait in the line outside."

Moving on and Up

In the early 1950s, when there were a handful of Eat'n Park locations and storing money under mattresses was nothing more than a memory, Larry Hatch and Bill Peters established an office on West Liberty Avenue above a soda and candy store. Since Larry was still employed by Isaly's, the office was staffed by Bill Peters, president, and Dorothy Carroll, who was the company's first administrative assistant. Dorothy was fiercely loyal to Larry and Bill and was instrumental in developing the early systems that kept the operations of the young company organized.

With growth and time, the company moved its offices to Banksville Road near the Eat'n Park restaurant. The next move took the company to a much larger distribution center in Vista Industrial Park in Robinson Township, a few miles west of downtown Pittsburgh. The center housed a few offices, and most of the property served as a distribution center for food supplies, as it still does today.

A Berry Good Idea

In 1954, Dwight D. Eisenhower was president of the United States; a young man from Tupelo, Mississippi, named Elvis Presley began his music career; Swanson introduced TV dinners; and Claire Moore – daughter of Larry Hatch – created a now-legendary pie for Eat'n Park.

Claire married Bob Moore, a high school math teacher, in July 1951. When the two returned from their honeymoon, Bob began working at Eat'n Park. Although he went on to serve the company for nearly 40 years, eventually as president, his father-in-law made him prove his worth – Bob's first job was that of grill man at the Dormont restaurant.

Tom Burress and Bob Moore worked the grill together.

A few years into his tenure, when Bob had risen to be a restaurant manager, he and company president Bill Peters took a road trip to Manner's Big Boy in Cleveland. The two had heard Manner's served a strawberry pie that had quickly become very popular, so they wanted to taste test for themselves.

The verdict: "Their pies were like Jell-O® with strawberries," Bob said. "Nothing special."

During the drive back to Pittsburgh, Bob told Bill that he was certain his wife could make a much better pie. Bill gave him the go ahead, hoping the pie would become a sales leader.

At the time, Claire was a 23-year-old mother of two who believed she had better things to do than bake strawberry pies. In fact, her response to her husband was a sarcastic, "Oh, great!"

From her little kitchen in the Moores' Scott Township home, Claire got to work. She began with a recipe from an old, worn-out cookbook and tried many variations to please the judges – her Scott Township neighbors. Pie after pie, their comments ranged from too sweet to too tart, too many strawberries to not enough strawberries. Finally, Claire came up with a balance of flavors that pleased the palates of all the judges.

We Love Strawberry Pie!
(stats from January 1 - June 30, 2022)

47,508 = **142,524**
strawberry pies sold   pounds of strawberries

79,544 = **39,772**
slices of   pounds of strawberries
strawberry pies sold

Claire Moore and her son Bill with their favorite strawberry pie

In 1954, the now classic Eat'n Park strawberry pie was born. Just as Claire created it, Eat'n Park's strawberry pie has always featured two pounds of fresh (never frozen) strawberries. The pie is such a guest favorite that, for years, it has been the focus of an advertising campaign called "The Merry Berry Month of May."

Interestingly, Claire Moore never made another strawberry pie once tasked to do so by her husband. She had said with a smile, "I know where to buy them now!"

Other Ideas

In the early days of Eat'n Park, the company dabbled in other business ventures. At one time, Eat'n Park owned three car washes, called Gas'n Glo, overseen by Larry Hatch's son-in-law Andy Hansen. It was a short-lived experiment, but the three provided a favorable return on investment when sold. The company also experimented with walk-up fast food in Oakland, downtown Pittsburgh, and Lawrenceville. None of the other business ventures achieved long-term success. The biggest variation was called Eaton's and was located on Banksville Road, near the Eat'n Park restaurant. Eaton's served sandwiches, pizza, and beer. According to Bob Moore, "We were out of our element, and the concept was a mistake."

Eaton's was a concept of Eat'n Park.

Moore Memories

Bob Moore is a beloved figure in the history of Eat'n Park. He earned respect for the knowledge he invested in the company and his nurturing style with team members. He began with the company as a grillman, and in 1987, Jim Broadhurst appointed him president. In 2002, Bob wrote the company history while recuperating from a broken ankle. Below are exact excerpts.

A MISTAKEN IDENTITY

When I was the supervisor, and we had seven or eight restaurants, **we felt a need for new managers**. I put on a campaign to recruit some of the assistant managers from Isaly's. I heard that the assistant at the Brookline Isaly's, by the name of Chester Parfitt, was very good, so off I went. When I went into the dairy store, I asked for the assistant manager. When he came out, I asked him if we could sit down and talk about his future. My selling point was that with Isaly's he had one chance in 80 (that is how many stores Isaly's had) of being promoted, but with Eat'n Park he had one chance in eight. He was sold, and I said, "Welcome to Eat'n Park, Ches." He then told me that Ches had been transferred the day before to the Great Southern Isaly's in Bridgeville, and his name was George Cassidy. Oh well, I liked him regardless of who he was, so I hired him and took off for Bridgeville. Then, after interviewing the real Ches Parfitt, he also came over to Eat'n Park. They both became good managers for us and stayed for a number of years. I always kidded Cassidy that I hired him by mistake.

EARLY PROMOTIONS

The **"Moonlight Special"** was served after 8:00 p.m. and consisted of a Big Boy, French fries, and a Coke. This was all for 89¢ and was for car service only.

At one time we gave out collectible stamps. I can't remember exactly how it worked, but each customer had a card and for every 50¢ spent they got a stamp to stick on the card. When the card was filled with 40 stamps, they could redeem it for $3.00 in food value. It really turned out to be too labor intensive, so we made an announcement that we were ending it, but would honor all cards, even partially filled ones. For years after, we would get cards for redemption. I think they must have found them in their attics.

We even had **Big Boy comic books** that were a monthly giveaway for a number of years.

We also ran chances on television sets in our outlying restaurants. Each Big Boy purchased entitled the customer to one chance.

By far, the most successful promotion was the **"Half Price" on Tuesday nights between 5:00-8:00 p.m.** The half price was on a Big Boy and milkshake. I can't remember the exact price, but it was somewhere around 40¢ total. Our dinner business was weak then, thus the 5:00-8:00 p.m. period, but this promotion was a real barnburner! We really worked over those three hours. The milkshakes were hand

dispensed. If you got a hard 2½ gallon tub of ice cream, you could hardly lift your arm the next day. This promotion was in the lot only and many customers came at 4:00 p.m., parked their cars, and opened up their newspapers and waited. You could have a full lot by 4:30 p.m. – most reading their newspapers. The promotion was a great success and really built our dinner trade.

INNOVATIONS ON TRACK

We got into electronic car service where the customer called in over a speaker. Fancy canopies over the cars kept them out of the weather while they placed their orders. They were a good idea and had many benefits over our original service. It did much to speed up service and the turnover of cars. The first electronic system was installed at #28 Edgeworth. Like other firsts in our history, the first order presented a problem. I was behind the switchboard operator when the first order came in from the back of the lot. This to us was an historical moment. I heard the customer say, "I would like to place an order..." – and then all we heard was a loud noise. I looked out in the lot and saw our problem. A train was running on the rails right behind our lot. We had to wait four or five minutes until the train passed by to get the rest of the order. Why didn't someone think of the train problem when we put in the electronic system?

MAKING ACCOMMODATIONS

#1 Saw Mill Run – our first restaurant, had no dressing rooms for employees, and it was necessary to go over to the gas station next door to change your clothes. This was all right, as the owner of the gas station was also our landlord.

Saw Mill Run was also the restaurant where someone had the idea to get the aroma from our barbeque and baked bean steam table to the outside lot. We thought this would give our car service customers a hunger for these items. We cut a hole in the outside wall and placed a fan in it to distribute the aromas. The only problem was that the steam table was right next to the fryer and grill. The fan not only distributed the sweet smell of ham barbeques, but also the grease from our grill and fryers. In a very short time, customers parked up against the building were coming in complaining that grease was going all over their windshields. Not one of our better ideas!

THE FLIP SIDE

Let's talk about the cooks. During the weekdays we seldom used daylight cooks. The manager handled the grill, fryers, and board with help, when needed, from a waitress. We called ourselves working managers. Except for the carhop, all the uniforms were leased from a company called White Linen. The cooks and management wore the same uniform and did not wear nametags. White short-sleeve shirt, white pants, white apron, and an oversea-type hat. One of the big jobs of the supervisor was to enforce the policy of wearing the hat on the front of the head with no hair showing. Most managers started out as cooks. On a busy night we would use two cooks and the manager to work the fryers, grill, and board. With no air conditioning, it was a really hot job. He was responsible for keeping his area clean at all times and for cleaning up after close. Remember that he and his cooking area were in full view of the customer at the counter. An example of how thrifty we were: the manager on daylight used one side of the apron and then the manager at night would reverse the same apron and wear the dirty side to the inside. Had to keep a low linen expense! Cooks were paid around $1 an hour.

Early exterior signage at the Whitehall restaurant reflected the service style of Eat'n Park restaurants.

The interior of restaurants was changed to accommodate the move from car service to in-restaurant dining.

2

The Growth Years
A New Vision

Jim Broadhurst was beginning his sixth year with Pittsburgh National Bank (now PNC). He had gone through the bank's Management Training Program, worked as a financial analyst, and was now a commercial lending officer and assistant vice president responsible for customers and prospects in Milwaukee,

Minneapolis, Chicago, and Pittsburgh. But more importantly for Jim's future, in addition to territories, lending officers' groups were assigned specialty areas, and the group Jim was assigned to were retailers and wholesalers, food companies, and restaurants.

"I really enjoyed getting to know the bank's Pittsburgh clients, as well as the prospective clients in the Midwest who had reason to bank in Pittsburgh," Jim remembers. "Food companies like Heinz®, Pillsbury®, Kraft Foods®, Consolidated Food®, Land O'Lakes®, and McDonald's were some of my favorite targets for developing new and expanding relationships for Pittsburgh National Bank. National restaurant chains were particularly good targets because of their desire to add banks to their credit facility in new markets where they were opening restaurants."

One of Jim's partners in his group offered his Eat'n Park account to Jim. "I jumped at the chance," Jim says. "While I knew nothing about Eat'n Park except that my wife, Suzy, used to hang out there with her boyfriend when she was a teenager, I was happy to add any new clients that would help me become more knowledgeable about the restaurant industry while helping them grow."

It was 1971, and Jim decided he needed to get to know these Eat'n Park people. He was told he should contact Bill Peters at the company, but when Jim reached out, Bill had recently suffered a heart attack and was out on medical leave.

"I found out Larry Hatch was the person I should be calling on, but there was no mention of Larry Hatch in our bank files," Jim says. "I made a cold call on Larry and said, 'I just want to see if there's anything we could be doing for you. We appreciate your store deposit accounts and would be happy to help finance your continued growth.'"

Larry told Jim that he had some restaurants that needed to be refurbished and remodeled. "I want to start with McKees Rocks," he said. "That's our highest volume restaurant, and I want to expand the dining room." At that time, because most of Eat'n Park's sales were the result of carhop service, inside dining space was limited to 7-10 stools and 10-12 booths in most locations.

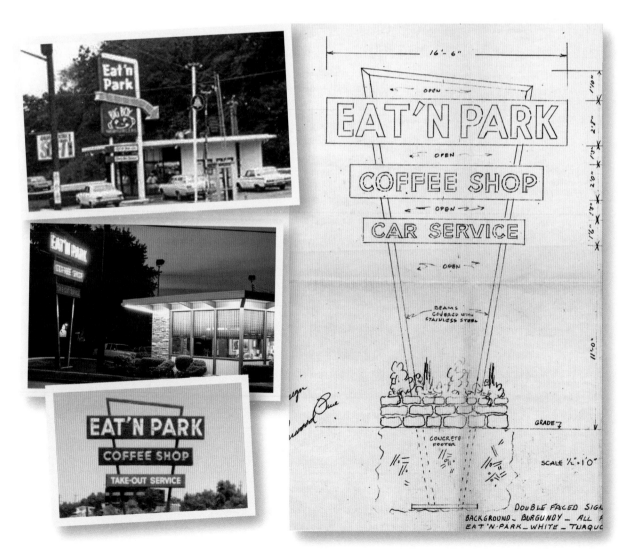

Larry and Jim coordinated a visit to the McKees Rocks Eat'n Park on an upcoming Saturday. That led to additional calls to Pittsburgh National Bank to gather financial information and establish a line of credit for Eat'n Park.

"We discussed his thoughts about eliminating car service in many of his investments," Jim remembers. The banker knew a change of that magnitude would require a large investment in bricks and mortar and expanded seating. "Over time, this would be very expensive," Jim says. "But I agreed that it was probably the correct long-term strategy."

One stumbling block was that Larry Hatch did not like having bank debt. But the company did not have adequate cash flow to finance the changes or to build additional restaurants. Dick Wright, a business owner, wanted to buy the company. Although Larry and Bill needed the cash, they refused his offer. But Larry saw a way to access Wright's capital without giving up ownership of the company. Larry and Dick agreed that the Richard Wright Corporation would finance building restaurants, and Eat'n Park would operate them, paying a fee to the Richard Wright Corporation.

Larry told Jim that he had some restaurants that needed to be refurbished and remodeled. "I want to start with McKees Rocks," he said. "That's our highest volume restaurant, and I want to expand the dining room."

Eventually, Dick Wright owned seven Eat'n Park restaurants. EPM, the partnership that Larry Hatch and Bill Peters created, owned more than 10 restaurants. "The income from these restaurants was restricted to payout to family, friends, and investors," relays Jim. "There was little cash flow available to finance the dining room expansions or build new restaurants.

"Larry was not afraid to try to improve things," Jim explains. "He wasn't afraid to take risks." He had experimented with other means of generating cash, including opening a large Eat'n Park in downtown Butler, north of Pittsburgh, and one-off ventures – Eaton's restaurant and Gas'n Glo car washes. None of the experiments proved to be the answer. "In fact, the growth rate of the business was stalled partially because of experimenting with new ideas," Jim says.

If Larry was to expand the renovation of restaurants beyond the McKees Rocks location, he would need a loan. Jim Broadhurst knew exactly where he could get one – Pittsburgh National Bank. As the restaurant owner and the banker began to work out the details of financing the restaurants' growth, Larry and Jim were gradually evolving into a well-balanced business team.

One July day in 1973, as Jim was wrapping up his work at the bank and preparing to leave on a family vacation, Larry called him. "I would like to hire a top financial person for our company and would appreciate any recommendations you would have." Jim told him he was leaving on a vacation but promised Larry several names when he returned the following week.

As promised, when Jim returned, he gave Larry the background of some people he thought were qualified to serve Eat'n Park in a finance position. Larry responded: "Well, what about you? You'd fit in perfectly." Jim, a little surprised, told Larry that he didn't think the opportunity was directed at him. Larry spelled out the details of what Jim's compensation would be, and it would far exceed what he was then earning. And Larry hinted that there may be more opportunities down the road.

The wheels began turning. Jim and his wife, Suzy, had two young sons, Jeff and Brooks (Mark arrived a few years later), and they were living in a small home in Mt. Lebanon. They were both still in their 20s. Jim was progressing nicely with his banking career, and Suzy was an elementary school teacher in the Baldwin-Whitehall School District. But this new opportunity had great promise. Should he stay with the sure thing or make a move into a new job with a different company in a completely different industry? Furthermore, Larry once had

Young Broadhurst sons, left to right: Mark, Jeff, and Brooks

mentioned that his four daughters – Betty, Claire, Eleanor, and Barb – owned the company, and Jim had not met them. This was a slight concern, but Jim was confident he could work effectively with the family owners.

Jim had a lot to think about. He loved his job at the bank, but the restaurant industry really intrigued him. As Suzy and Jim discussed all the pros and cons, they became more excited about the opportunity.

Jim then reached out to his most trusted friends for advice. Among them was Lester Hamburg, owner of Hamburg Brothers and a member of Pittsburgh National Bank's Board of Directors. Jim explained the situation to Lester. He shared that Larry Hatch had given most of the controlling interest of the company to his four daughters, whom he did not know. In addition, posing even more of a potential challenge, three of the daughters' husbands worked for the company. What if they did not get along? But Larry had offered Jim a five-year guarantee, and in five years he was going to be in much more favorable financial shape, and because of the responsibilities of his job, he would certainly expand his resume.

Lester listened intently, then gave Jim his advice. "Well, I don't think I want you to leave the bank. I'd hate to see you go, but," he said, "you're only going to be 34 in five years, and it's not like you can't find another job with your background. Pittsburgh National has a lot of respect for you. But this is something that broadens you, and you're going to learn a lot from moving into the top financial position. You'll be the chief financial officer of the company."

Jim decided to make the change, and what a change it would be for both him and Suzy.

~~~~~~

Jim had a lot to think about. He loved his job at the bank, but the restaurant industry really intrigued him. As Jim and Suzy discussed all the pros and cons, they became more excited about the opportunity.

~~~~~~

The Dawning of a New Era

On October 1, 1973, his first day on the job, Jim Broadhurst, executive vice president and treasurer, walked into the Eat'n Park distribution center at Vista Industrial Park. In addition to the warehouse and business operations, the offices of Larry Hatch and Bill Peters were located here. Since Bill was out on a medical leave, Larry instructed Jim to move into his office, causing Jim to wonder about the likelihood of Bill returning to the company.

While Jim was getting settled inside, outside in the field, the transition from carhop service to dining-room service was just beginning. Carhop service was still the largest revenue generator. Carhops were more than a style of service; they were entertainment, they were gathering spots, they were a lifestyle. The restaurants would be changing service and – even more challenging – they would be changing mindsets.

A New Start

Once Jim became an employee of Eat'n Park in 1973, he never looked back. "I never second-guessed the decision," he says. "I knew what I had to do, and I had confidence in the industry. I knew the industry. I knew we were capable of growing the business, both with new units and larger remodels. My first impression of the three sons-in-law in the business, Bob Moore, Chuck Veazey, and Andy Hansen, was very positive, so, I jumped in with both feet."

Jim's first challenge was to try to get the business in order from a financial standpoint. He knew firsthand that's what bankers expected. He also made some staffing adjustments and added a little more structure to the organization.

Jim's research into the company actually began before his first day on the job. Without anyone knowing, he and Suzy did some undercover work. "We went out at all times of the day and evening to enjoy a meal at Eat'n Park restaurants."

While the undercover diners made some pleasant discoveries, they also discovered things that inspired improvements. "On one of our first visits to a restaurant," Suzy remembers, "we walked in, and someone dropped chicken bones from their dinner under their stool at the counter, and no one had cleaned them up! We just shook our heads. There was work to be done!"

At a different location, Suzy and Jim entered the restaurant and found a bucket and two mops blocking a section of seating to prevent guests from entering. "Jim was looking around trying to figure out what to do," Suzy says. "Someone yelled out from the back, 'Oh you can't go there. That section is closed.'"

In Jim's judgment, there were many obvious changes to make right away. He chose to start slowly and build, but he never forgot about the other needed changes – changes like adding greeters to welcome guests and show them to their seats, and never seating a guest at a dirty table. Jim believed the managers could benefit from additional training – they were great at cooking but didn't have experience training their staff or focusing on the guest experience. But his priority was ensuring all restaurants were operating in the black.

Once Jim was onboard, his restaurant visits were no longer undercover. With Bill Peters out on medical leave, Larry Hatch accompanied Jim on a few of his restaurant visits. On one visit, they discovered a bucket on a counter stool, carefully positioned to catch water dripping from the ceiling.

"It appeared it had been that way for a day or two," Jim recalls. "It was obvious that the company lacked a sense of urgency to fix problem areas and service deficiencies. We both realized the need to spend some money to make some changes."

Larry became very stressed when he discovered problems, and he saw in Jim someone who could lead the necessary changes. With Jim in a leadership position, Larry could return to doing what he was comfortable with – working from his office, not being on the road visiting restaurants.

The restaurant visits also enabled Jim to observe the operations. "It became very obvious that the leader in the place was back in the kitchen all the time," Jim says. "The managers were respected in the restaurants because they were the best cooks, not because they were the best at taking care of the guests." Almost all the managers grew up in the back of the house where the kitchen was located, not in the front where the dining room was.

Once Bill Peters was feeling better, he would accompany Jim on visits. "Bill didn't believe in calling ahead to the restaurants," Jim remembers. "He liked to enter through the back door and go right into the kitchen area, right to the grill area. He believed that was the best way to see if something was wrong. He was focused on systems and procedures, but surprise visits could stress the employees, even if they were doing a good job."

After Bill's retirement, Jim's restaurant visits continued, sometimes accompanied by Bob Moore or a district supervisor. "It was a great way to learn the heartbeat of the business. Bob was very supportive," Jim says. "The staff trusted Bob, so they started off trusting me. When I look back on those early days, I realize how much easier Bob made it for me. He was gracious to introduce me on occasion as his boss, and it gave me credibility."

By observing Bill's and Bob's styles of conducting restaurant visits, Jim developed his own style. "It didn't take me long to learn that if you want to have a meaningful conversation with a manager," Jim says, "you'd better call ahead. The managers needed time to prepare. At that time, most were cooking, too. They may have been the only cook on that shift."

"We made those people service supervisors. They were responsible for the development of the people who were on the floor serving guests."

— Jim Broadhurst

Eventually, as Jim gained more authority, he was able to address the need for an emphasis on hospitality and service skills. He knew that to achieve his vision, he would need to build a winning team. He started by building on the strengths already in place.

"I picked the locations where there was a handful of people with a good service mentality," he explains. "We made those people waitress supervisors, and we trained them to be service supervisors. They were responsible for the development of the people who were on the floor serving guests."

Jim also was interested in what the competition was experiencing. "My first memory of Eat'n Park being significant in our family is when I was in elementary school," explains Brooks Broadhurst, Suzy and Jim's middle son. "We would drive through the parking lots of all of the competitors and count how many cars were in their lot. That's how we could tell if Elby's, Denny's, Winky's, or any of those different places were doing more business than us. We did it all the time. And when we finally got to Eat'n Park, we would park the farthest from the front door, leaving the better parking spots for guests."

Advertisement from the *Pittsburgh Press Roto Magazine* introducing waitress supervisors in the mid-1970s

Service Evolves

Part of the waitress supervisors' job was to build self-confidence and consistency in the servers. They needed to understand that they now were empowered. They could, for example, stop an order from leaving the kitchen if it wasn't the way the guest ordered it. Managers couldn't overrule the servers because the directive from Jim and Bob was to put more emphasis on the guest and the guest experience.

"I always believed we should err on the side of giving better service and generous portions," Jim remembers. "I was confident that, if we took care of our guests, our sales would continue to grow, and we would meet or exceed our financial projections. The company had never experienced a loss, and the management team in every restaurant was very good at meeting or exceeding their food-cost and payroll goals."

Eventually, as the company's footprint changed, so, too, did the composition of its workforce as men took on new roles. There were no longer waitresses, there were servers. Waitress supervisors became service supervisors. Hostesses became greeters.

_____

Something to Smile About

At age 16, Trice Whitely arrived at the Monongahela Eat'n Park as a less-than-seasoned server. "My experience was with the local bingo," Trice laughs. "My father was a fireman, so I would go to the New Eagle bingo every Thursday night and serve. There were no child labor laws back then," she adds with a smile.

Trice's first day with Eat'n Park was November 27, 1973. It's a day she remembers well. "We automatically served water to all our guests, and I emptied an entire tray of water on my first guest! I'm still not sure why I returned to the restaurant the next day," she says laughing.

As high school graduation approached, Trice was unsure what she wanted to do. While she weighed her options, she continued working at the Monongahela restaurant.

John Vichie was the district supervisor who oversaw the Monongahela restaurant at the time. He visited the restaurant to tell the manager that he needed a waitress to become a waitress supervisor at the Washington, Pennsylvania, restaurant. He asked if the restaurant manager, Mike Harris, had anyone up to the task. The manager replied, "Well, I think Trice would do a good job."

John's response was immediate: "She doesn't smile enough."

"That was a huge learning experience for me," Trice recalls. "I conditioned myself to make sure I was smiling. They took a chance on me, and I transferred to the Washington restaurant. Training became a passion of mine," Trice continues. "They just kept asking me to come back and open the new restaurants."

TRICE WHITELY
Washington, Pa.

The mid-to-late 1970s was a period of rapid growth with several restaurants opening every year, making it clear that there was a need for someone to train employees at each location. Gail Ulrich, a trainer from the Aliquippa restaurant, was chosen to lead the company-wide training effort. "Gail was an outstanding team member who was well respected, and we needed someone who could provide leadership to formalize the training initiative," Jim Broadhurst explains. As director of training and development, Gail put in place a structure that launched the company's first formal training program.

Eventually, as Gail was promoted to vice president of training and development, Trice became the director of training for the Eat'n Park Restaurant Division, until her retirement in 2021. In addition to training Eat'n Park restaurant team members, she trained team members for Hello Bistro and for both The Porch at Schenley and The Porch at Siena.

Trice not only trained, she also learned. And Jim, a fellow member of the Eat'n Park Class of 1973, created an educational opportunity for which Trice will be forever grateful.

"Jim and Suzy, both Penn State alumni, worked closely with the university to develop an online hospitality associate degree program," Trice explains. "I'm very proud that I'm a graduate of Penn State with an associate degree in Hotel, Restaurant and Institutional Management, and I am the first person to graduate from the program through Penn State's World Campus. And darn it, at 50 years old, didn't I go to Penn State and walk across the stage to get that degree, and didn't Jim Broadhurst give it to me in his role as chairman of the Penn State Board of Trustees!"

John Vichie would be pleased with the smile on Trice's face.

The Role of Gender

Up until the late 1970s, society often drew gender lines for employment. It was common to see help-wanted ads in newspapers divided into those for women and others for men. At that time in the restaurant industry, usually managers were men, waitresses were women. Jim, however, was deeply troubled by this perceived gender line.

"I saw a female team member I thought was really impressive," Jim remembers. "I said to the district supervisor, 'This person would be good in management. I've talked to her a couple of times, and I like the way she thinks.' And the district supervisor responded, 'No, she'll never become a manager. When an order comes in from the distributor, she can't put those big boxes up on the shelves.' I'll never forget that moment," Jim continues. "I remember exactly where I was when I heard

GIRLS

Refined, pleasant personable; age 21 to 30, for desirable position as waitresses at Pittsburgh's Eat 'N Park Restaurant. Free uniforms, meal allowances, good wages, restaurant completely air conditioned. Full and part time positions available. Applicants interviewed Friday evening 7-9:30; Saturday afternoon 2-4, at

EAT N' PARK

2209 Saw Mill Run Blvd.

An early help-wanted ad

that if you can't pick up a big, heavy box and put it on a shelf, you can't be a manager."

Moving forward, Jim made certain big boxes did not stand in the way of big dreams. Today, he celebrates the success of the career paths of Trice Michaels, Mercy Senchur, JoAnn Walk, and so many other women who began their careers as servers with Eat'n Park and advanced to senior managerial positions and, in doing so, proved that leading is not about size, stature, or gender.

"I remember exactly where I was when I heard that if you can't pick up a big, heavy box and put it on a shelf, you can't be a manager."

— Jim Broadhurst

Change at the Top

"From the time I was hired in 1973 until 1984, I couldn't have been more pleased with the success of the company and my relationship with Larry Hatch," Jim reflects. Everything Larry promised Jim when he made the job offer had come to pass. "He promoted me to president in 1975, well before I expected, and he passed along the responsibilities of overseeing marketing and selecting real estate sites in the late '70s and early '80s."

The two had occasional differences of opinion, but their relationship stayed strong. "I admired his vision, his hard work in his 60s and 70s, and his thoughtfulness and generosity," Jim says. "He had a soft heart but was not able to express those feelings without becoming emotional, and so he avoided doing so at all costs. He was a brilliant man but very uncomfortable interacting in public settings."

Jim and Larry met every day when both were in the office, and both men looked forward to those meetings. "He had become my good friend and mentor," Jim says. "He was a great visionary, and I was able to help him bring his vision to reality."

As years went by, Eat'n Park continued to build restaurants in a much wider footprint. The company also remodeled existing restaurants that needed to be upgraded.

In 1980, Larry gave Suzy and Jim some of his family's stock. He told Jim that he would move toward having the Broadhurst family become a 10% shareholder. "Bill Peters also needed to approve that gift because his family's interest would be diluted," Jim explains. "I was grateful that the two principal shareholders appreciated my positive impact on the company."

One early morning in 1984, Jim knocked on Larry's office door. "Mornings were the best time to have personal conversations with Larry about important subjects," Jim remembers. "I decided to talk with him about his family's long-term interest in owning the company. I had heard him comment occasionally about corporations like Heinz expressing an interest in Eat'n Park or that his family might want to sell the company in the future."

Jim expressed to Larry that if he was thinking about selling the company, he would be very interested in attempting to make a favorable offer for the business. Jim knew that Larry's daughters were the majority shareholders, but he was fairly sure that it would be Larry who would decide the price and terms of the sale.

Larry viewed Jim as the logical person to buy the company. He recognized that Jim had assembled a strong team, both by promoting from within and recruiting additional expertise from the outside. He knew that it was largely because of Jim's leadership and his new team that the company's sales and earnings were steadily improving.

Shortly after buying the company, Jim promoted Bob Moore to president.

"He couldn't have been nicer or more considerate when he expressed interest in exploring a sale to Suzy and me," Jim remembers.

Without taking more than five minutes to think about the price, Larry gave Jim a number that was fair and based on the book value of the company. "He generously offered me enough time to explore partner interests and financing arrangements through a bank," says Jim. "I thanked him, told him I just wanted our family without partners to be the purchasers and was going to count on Pittsburgh National Bank to take a chance on a very good client and former employee with no money!"

As Jim left the office, Larry wished him luck. Jim was excited and hopeful. It hadn't occurred to him yet that he and Suzy were about to take a significant risk. "I do think I left Larry with a slight smile on his face, thinking about the risk he took some 35 years earlier in 1949," Jim says.

Jim reached out to his longtime friend Tom O'Brien who was a top executive with Pittsburgh National Bank, at the time. Since the stock that Suzy and Jim would be buying would put them in the position of owning more than 50% of the company's outstanding voting shares, Tom agreed to finance the purchase with terms favorable to both the Hatch and Broadhurst families.

On November 1, 1984, the deal was done.

"Everything went so smoothly," Jim recalls, "that I decided not to announce the change in ownership. Nothing would change in how the business would run because Larry would still come in most days, and Bob Moore would remain vice president of operations until I promoted him to president."

Making Dollars Count

After the purchase, Jim made it a priority to strengthen the company's financial performance. "We bought back seven Eat'n Park restaurants that were owned by the Richard Wright Corporation, our only franchises, and we eliminated the franchise model," Jim explains. Jim also directed that profits were to be reinvested in the company, and as a result, the company, for the first time, had a strong balance sheet and capital that was growing.

3

Another Evolution
People, Places, and Perspectives

The 1970s were a decade of tremendous growth for Eat'n Park Restaurants, with the first expansion outside of Pennsylvania, in Boardman, Ohio. Supporting rapid growth required expanding the team, and one of the key new hires occurred in 1977 when Dave Wohleber came on board. Dave had been a senior accountant with Price Waterhouse, and he and Jim had met years earlier through the Jaycees, the Junior Chamber of Commerce.

"I had kind of been pushing Jim to let us do a proposal for Eat'n Park," Dave remembers. "He called me up one day and said, 'I'd like to have breakfast with you.' I thought he was going to ask to have Price Waterhouse do the audit. But when we met, he said, 'I'd like you to join us as our treasurer.' I almost fell off my chair – literally. I didn't see that coming at all."

"I was delighted when Dave accepted my offer," Jim says. "While we had an outstanding controller in Jim Cavrak, we needed a CPA from a large financial accounting firm who could provide me with sound advice in conservative business practices and successfully secure appropriate financing for growth. Dave was a winner!"

Dave Wohleber's expertise was essential to growing the company.

Dave's accounting experience included an expertise in taxation, a knowledge that was critically important to a growing, private company. Over the years, Dave earned promotions, ultimately serving as chief financial officer. "In the years I was CFO, the company never lost money. We never had that problem," Dave relates. "We planned ahead, and we had a bank line of credit with PNC, who was a really good business partner."

Dave built on the structure Jim Broadhurst had started, introduced more processes and discipline, including having the general managers of each restaurant develop their own annual budget. "We encouraged them to find out what was going on in the community," Dave explains. "Is there a new office complex going in down the street? Why is there a 'For Sale' sign on the property across the way? Is there a competitor restaurant coming into the neighborhood? These are all things that would affect the financial plan."

Strong finances were essential to fund the rapid growth.

Moving in a New Direction

In the early 1980s Ketchum MacLeod & Grove was the largest advertising agency in Pittsburgh. It was in the heart of downtown Pittsburgh, in Four Gateway Center. Ketchum's offices were opulent, and the working atmosphere was equally notable.

Eat'n Park was a client of Ketchum's, and the administrative assistant who supported the Eat'n Park account was Kathy James (then Barrett), a young woman from Dormont. Kathy was responsible for greeting visitors from Eat'n Park, scheduling meetings, and answering their phone calls which – most often – were from either Bill McKinsey, the head of marketing, or Jim Broadhurst, president.

When the pair would arrive at Ketchum for a meeting, "I had to remind myself: McKinsey was marketing, Broadhurst was president," Kathy recalls with a laugh. "McKinsey looked presidential with his beautiful white hair; Jim looked so young and like a kid."

With every interaction, Jim was growing more impressed with Kathy's skills and her style in dealing with people. He was impressed by her tenacity in tracking down answers to his questions and solutions to his concerns, and he appreciated her always pleasant demeanor.

In 1982 after meeting with Kathy over lunch, Jim offered her the opportunity to join Eat'n Park as his executive assistant. But Kathy needed some time to make her decision. She loved working downtown and loved Ketchum's swanky offices. The job with Jim would be in the suburbs, and the office would be a bit different from Ketchum's – it was in a warehouse in an industrial park.

After considerable thought, Kathy accepted the job. "My first day, I drove out the Parkway West and got off at the Crafton exit," Kathy remembers. "At the stop sign, I looked across the road, and there were cows and horses grazing in the pasture! I burst into tears and said, 'I have made the biggest mistake of my life.'"

Fast forward 41 years and Kathy says, "I absolutely made the right decision. I've seen many changes over the years – two moves of our headquarters, diversification of the company, incredible growth, and a pandemic. Through it all," she continues, "Jim and Suzy have always kept that culture of caring for our team members and our communities. And Jeff, Brooks, and Mark continue to live those values. I'm so proud and privileged to work for Jim and to be a part of this amazing company."

"Kathy is an exceptional team member, but more importantly, she's an extraordinary person," Jim reflects. "She has very high expectations of her own performance and is driven to exceed them – and always does so with a smile. Little did I know 40 years ago that I was hiring someone who would become indispensable in so many facets of my life."

Kathy and Jim are close collaborators.

Becoming a Family

With the ending of car service, Eat'n Park restaurants became totally dine-in restaurants, primarily coffee shops. But that wasn't the vision Jim Broadhurst had – he wanted the restaurants to be a place where families would dine together.

So, how would Eat'n Park transition to a family restaurant?

In 1980, Jim had attended a gathering at his church, and the guest speaker was a representative of Family Communications, a company formed by Fred Rogers in 1971. Fred was the focus of a program produced by WQED-TV, the PBS affiliate in Pittsburgh, called *Mister Rogers' Neighborhood*. Everything Family Communications produced – TV episodes, books, videos – reflected Fred's philosophy of helping children grow as confident, competent, and caring human beings.

The speaker's message resonated with Jim: Children as confident, competent, caring human beings. Certainly, that was something Eat'n Park could embrace. But how?

Jim reached out to Family Communications. Basil Cox, then general manager of the company, remembers the call. "Jim said he admired Fred, and he admired *Mister Rogers' Neighborhood*. He wondered if we could help him make Eat'n Park more family friendly."

With inspiration from Fred Rogers and Family Communications, Eat'n Park introduced specially designed children's menus.

In the restaurant industry, children weren't desired guests. "They make a lot of noise, create a huge mess, and they don't spend money," Basil explains. "It's hard to see the value of kids in restaurants. But Jim was a big believer in families. He thought it was very important that Eat'n Park should be welcoming to families with small children."

Jim and Basil discussed how a restaurant might contribute to strengthening the core of children and families and how restaurants could serve as a type of family-gathering space where adults and children interact throughout their meal.

Basil and his Family Communications colleague Cathy Droz began working on ideas that would help families communicate with each other by engaging them in an activity while they were at Eat'n Park. The roll out of activities began in September 1980. "We did kids' menus as flip books," Basil remembers, "and we did placemats that had activities on them, things parents and kids could enjoy together."

Changing the restaurants' emphasis to be family focused required a change in service, too. Many restaurant team members had started as carhops, serving primarily young adults. The coffee shop days required still another shift. But nothing to this point was as big a departure from what servers knew. "We did some training," Basil remembers, "explaining the philosophy of *Mister Rogers' Neighborhood* to Eat'n Park servers."

The term, "family restaurant," was not used frequently in the early 1980s. "Jim's approach was kind of visionary because that was an era of coffee shops. Or they were family-style restaurants where the food would be served in one big platter in the middle, and you'd share it. Jim was one of the earliest to think, 'Wait a minute. There are legs in this idea of family restaurants,'" Basil says.

Jim wanted every part of the Eat'n Park experience to be as family oriented as possible. Instead of a table with two chairs, booths were introduced to accommodate larger parties. Menu designs depicted families on the cover.

The Squirrel Hill restaurant was depicted in a menu from the 1980s, showcasing Eat'n Park's move to family dining.

Eat'n Park
RESTAURANTS
"We Specialize in Goodness"

Jim's vision combined with Family Communications' expertise blended to successfully move Eat'n Park away from coffee shops and toward family restaurants. The term 'family restaurant' eventually became a category in the industry, as more and more restaurants embraced the approach.

Basil's contributions to transitioning Eat'n Park from a coffee shop to a family restaurant so impressed Jim that he recruited him to join the team. "Basil had a strong marketing background; he had great instincts," Jim remembers. In March 1984, Basil moved from working in *Mister Rogers' Neighborhood* to Eat'n Park's neighborhood. He began as director of marketing, and in March 1993, he became president of the Eat'n Park Restaurants.

A Personal Touch

Larry Hatch and Jim had different philosophies about how opening days for new restaurants should be managed. "When Larry opened restaurants, he wanted a lot of people to be there," Jim remembers. "I thought we should let our new team members gain some confidence – not overwhelm them with too many people."

There were times when the preparation of the new buildings came close to intersecting with the first guests arriving. This was certainly true for the opening of the New Castle Eat'n Park. The team – including Suzy and Jim – were up all night before the next day's opening. "People would be putting the furniture in," Jim says, "or they'd be painting the building. We'd run out and buy the paintings and hang them in the restaurant."

"That was being done as guests were coming in the door," Suzy adds. "We'd tell the guests to be careful not to bump up against the walls because the paint was still wet!"

As is tradition when new Eat'n Park locations open, the evening before the New Castle opening, the Broadhursts invited the new management team and their spouses to a special dinner at a neighborhood restaurant. "Our leadership team joined us," Jim remembers. "We wanted to get to know them personally and thank them for all the hard work they did getting the restaurant ready to open." This is a tradition that the company's leadership continues today.

After long, exhausting days preparing for the opening, the team opened the doors to the New Castle restaurant. "Claire Moore and I were the welcomers," Suzy says with a chuckle. "We handed each guest a flower as they entered the new restaurant. I guess you could say we were the first hostesses."

"We'd tell the guests to be careful not to bump up against the walls because the paint was still wet!"

— Suzy Broadhurst

Freshly Baked Smiles

Jim Broadhurst stopped at a Fuddruckers® restaurant while traveling in Columbus, Ohio, in the mid-1980s. He noticed that they had a bakery where they made hamburger buns.

"It occurred to me that we could do a much better job by having a visible bakery," Jim remembers. "We could do breakfast items, dessert items, we could bake different things in the bakery and have it visible in the front of the restaurant."

Jim's vision included the smell of products baking in the oven. "When the products were baking, I wanted the smell to go through the bakery ceiling and back into the lobby of the restaurant."

As Jim drove back to Pittsburgh, he grew more and more excited about the idea of bakeries in the restaurants. "It was like it was almost done," he says, "because nobody was going to talk me out of doing it. I thought it was really going to enhance the quality of products."

With each mile came an idea. "I started thinking about trips Suzy and I made to her grandmother's in New Wilmington. We loved to visit the Tavern Restaurant there that had the most delicious sweet rolls. So, Suzy and I went back to New Wilmington to have lunch at the Tavern to sample the sweet rolls again. We went home excited to have John Vichie, our director of product development, create our own honey bun."

Jim also had memories of a bakery when he was growing up in Titusville. "They had a sugar cookie with white icing and a smiley face drawn in green icing," he remembers. "I would stop in Warner's Bakery every day on my way home from elementary school to buy one of those cookies. My mother would give me a nickel – not a dime – so I could buy only one cookie."

Titusville was home to Warner's Bakery, where young Jimmy purchased a smiling sugar cookie every day on his way home from school.

Although adding bakeries to the restaurants was a mouth-watering idea, Jim realized his team lacked something critical – knowledge of how to operate a bakery. It was time for another visit to Warner's Bakery.

"I visited with Ellsworth 'Pop' Warner, an old friend who I knew from the 50s. He owned the bakery and was always so nice to me. I told him we were going to put bakeries in our restaurants," Jim says. "I asked him if I could send somebody up to learn how to run a bakery. We'd have a team member live in Titusville for several months and work for Warner's, and Eat'n Park would pay the salary. That sounded awfully good to Mr. Warner."

Jim envisioned the team member would learn how to make a variety of bakery products, then return to Pittsburgh with product ideas and the knowledge to roll out the bakeries.

"Pop" Warner was in full agreement and was happy to offer his recipes.

When Jim was driving home from Titusville, his excitement continued to build, so he stopped at the Sewickley Eat'n Park to settle himself. He went to the back of the restaurant and found the assistant manager, someone he did not know.

"I told her who I was and asked if she had a couple of minutes to sit down with me," Jim explains. "And we just sat and started chatting. We were a few minutes into the conversation when I asked my usual questions when I'm getting to know someone: 'What do you do when you're not working? What are your hobbies?' She said, 'I love to bake.'"

Jim struggled to contain his delight about such a fortuitous encounter. "I knew this was going to be a great opportunity for her and her career and good for the restaurants, too," Jim remembers.

Barb Kiehl and Carol Perclavalle were Eat'n Park's first bakers.

When Jim returned to the office, he ran the idea of bakeries past some of his key people. They were all receptive to the idea. Jim returned to the Sewickley restaurant and again talked with the assistant manager whose name he now knew, Barb Kiehl. He shared his idea for bakeries and for sending someone to Titusville for a few months to learn the bakery business. He explained that it would be a good opportunity for her, it would lead to other avenues, and the company would pay all her expenses.

The assistant manager rose to the occasion.

Three months later, Barb returned to Pittsburgh. Jim decided to introduce bakeries at two of the restaurants to start, including Barb's home restaurant, Sewickley. In September of 1985, as additional bakeries were being added, Barb went to those restaurants and trained the team members. "We were doing a lot of things from scratch," Jim explains, "so she had to show them how to make the dough, roll it out, and cut it; she had to show them every step for every product."

For the employees of Eat'n Park

Spring 1986

WE'RE ROLLING OUT A FRESH IDEA

Sweet'n Fresh. Our honeybun. Dinnertime, it's our treat. Hot from the oven every day, those golden, cinnamon swirls keep the honey warm and cozy.

No, this isn't an excerpt from a steamy novel. Rather it's from a poster in Eat'n Park's hot new bakeries.

The customers and employees at four restaurants are already enjoying the experience, and the rest have it to look forward to.

The Bakery at Eat'n Park first opened at the Sewickley restaurant (#28) in early September. South Hills Village (#35) rolled theirs out in early November. Altoona (#46) and New Stanton (#37) started baking in March. Business at all is doing great; in fact, it is exceeding original expectations.

Mmm . . . check out that new bakery!

see two display cases in the lobby. A refrigerated case is filled with whole strawberry, cream and fruit pies. Scrumptious! The second, not refrigerated, contains a tempting assortment of rolls, muffins and smiley-face cookies frosted in six different colors.

Through glass windows into the Bakery, the customer catches enticing glimpses of

installed in 10-15 restaurants. Eventually, all of the restaurants will be serving bakery products.

As Eat'n Park continues to move forward and grow, the Bakery at Eat'n Park will be one of the innovations that allow it to continue to occupy its pre-eminent position as the leading full-service restaurant chain in

The bakeries began selling the smiley cookies of Jim's youth, as well as the Boston brown bread his mother used to make, and the honey buns like those from the restaurant near Suzy's grandmother's home. "And, of course," Jim says, "we had to include the grilled stickies we enjoyed in college following late night parties. We took things we knew were popular in different places, and we tweaked them a bit."

The bakery products were popular with guests, and no one would have guessed the effect that little round cookie was going to have.

Suzy and Jim's memories helped to inspire some of the items in Eat'n Park bakeries.

———————

A Bold Move

From the time Jim Broadhurst joined the team in 1973 through 1980, Eat'n Park Restaurants experienced a growth spurt. The space at the Distribution Center at Vista Industrial Park in Robinson Township was growing more and more crowded. Warehouse space was at a premium because as the number of restaurants grew, the amount of storage space required also grew. Staff members were sharing office space, but even that wasn't enough. It was time for a change.

Less than a few miles from the Distribution Center was an area of Robinson Township that Jim thought showed promise for development. At that time, there was a Giant Eagle grocery store and a Murphy Mart variety store. The former farmland had recently had its first traffic light installed – a clear harbinger of growth. There was talk of additional development, including a strip mall and a multi-screen theater.

There was a corner property adjoining the shopping center on Route 60 and Park Manor Drive in Robinson Township that Jim thought would be perfect for an attractive office building with an Eat'n Park restaurant on the first floor. "The site was beautiful with plenty of parking space to accommodate both our restaurant and an office building," Jim remembers. "I was certain this property and its location were perfect to support the company's next 20 years of growth and development. We could enjoy a large conference room for hosting our team members for training and our first test kitchen for developing menu items."

There was just one problem: the property owners did not want to sell it to a restaurant chain.

One of the two principals agreed to meet with Jim to discuss the property further. "We met on a Sunday," Jim explains. "During the meeting, I described our vision for the new office building with a very attractive Eat'n Park restaurant on the first floor. We envisioned a first-of-its-kind, two-story atrium in the midst of our guests dining in the restaurant. I also told him that we had decided to use his favorite architects to do the rendering for the new building."

By knowing the architects, the property owner would have the opportunity to view the renderings before they were presented to the Robinson Township Planning Commission. "That was probably the biggest selling point to subsequently approving our proposal. I was extremely grateful when he gave us the go ahead to buy his property."

But Larry Hatch was not on board.

The purchase price was a great deal of money, and Larry was not happy. His feelings were so strong that he shared them with Jim's executive team at a reception the night before the opening of the restaurant. "I felt let down by Larry's remarks," Jim says. "But all was forgotten when the restaurant opened as #1 in sales.

"Because of Larry's strong feelings, we decided to lease the second-floor space to Chrysler Corporation for five years," Jim explains. "That helped from a revenue standpoint." So, for five additional years the company's corporate office remained at the Distribution Center.

Jim knew the parcel in Robinson Township was perfect for a new restaurant and headquarters to house the expanding company.

Jim views those five years as a critical time in the company's history. "During that period of time, there was a whole transitioning of the company and a totally different framework from what it was before," he explains. "We were starting to develop the support services we needed; we were continuing to hire some really talented folks."

The Robinson Township Eat'n Park restaurant opened in 1981. As planned, five years later, on June 6, 1986, the new Eat'n Park headquarters opened on the floor above the restaurant. Jim moved the company office out of the Distribution Center to Park Manor Drive. It was a move of less than two miles, but it would open the door to a way of doing business that was lightyears ahead.

Operating with Passion

At age 18, Mercy Senchur didn't know anything about Pittsburgh. It was 1986, and she had moved to the city from Michigan. With previous experience limited to working as a cocktail waitress and in an ice cream shop, Mercy secured a position as a server with the Dormont Eat'n Park restaurant. Her sister Suzie worked there, and Mercy was counting on her to teach her what she needed to know about working in the restaurant.

After only a year on the job, Bill Charles, a manager, saw Mercy's potential and promoted her to service supervisor. "It set me on my path of setting goals," she says.

In 1990, another manager, Jeff Dean, asked Mercy to enter Eat'n Park's management training program. She worked for several locations over the next four years, serving as assistant manager or manager. After being named a general manager, Mercy was in line to open the Irwin Eat'n Park, an opportunity she was looking forward to because it was close to her home. And then she received a call.

"Chuck Sites, who was then a district supervisor, called me and said, 'Hey, Mercy, there's an opportunity that opened up at the Robinson Eat'n Park as a general manager.' I told him I was supposed to open a brand-new Eat'n Park as a general manager in Irwin. He told me to take the weekend to think about it and call him Monday morning at 7:00."

Mercy spent the weekend comparing the opportunities at Irwin and Robinson Township, including the lengthy commute she would have between her home in Irwin and the Robinson restaurant. She knew what she needed to do. On Monday, she called Chuck and told him she decided to take the Irwin opportunity.

"Chuck said to me, 'I'm really glad you took the time to think about it over the weekend. I'll see you at Robinson next Tuesday morning for orientation.' And I said, 'But Chuck, you said this was my decision, that I had a choice.' Chuck's response was, 'Yeah, you did, but you made the wrong one.'"

So, on the designated Tuesday, Mercy began a new assignment as general manager at the Robinson Township Eat'n Park. It was the largest Eat'n Park, and the corporate headquarters was located on the floor above the restaurant.

Over four years, Mercy's talents for managing a restaurant were witnessed daily by the corporate office team. In 1998, she was promoted to regional director, moving from overseeing one restaurant to overseeing all restaurants in a designated territory. She was the first woman to hold that position.

On a day-to-day basis, Mercy focused on setting standards and improving efficiency from unit to unit so that the restaurants could be as consistent as possible. After eight years, she was promoted to regional vice president, and as she gained more responsibilities, advanced to vice president, then senior vice

Mercy Senchur carved a path from server to chief operating officer of Eat'n Park's Restaurant Division.

president. Ultimately, Mercy was appointed chief operating officer of the Restaurant Division.

The unlikely rise of the new girl in town who walked to her job as a server because she didn't have a car to the senior executive overseeing nearly 70 restaurants and more than 5,000 team members, is something Mercy appreciates every day.

"I'm grateful to work for a company that has been so well run for so many years. I want to be a good steward of the culture that was developed."

"Team members can look to Mercy as an inspiration," Jeff Broadhurst says. "She's smart and driven, and her experience demonstrates that we look for opportunities for our team members' career growth."

A Memorable Negotiation

Site selection, whether for a corporate headquarters or a restaurant, has been an essential element in Eat'n Park's success. Dave Shaw, Eat'n Park's retired vice president of real estate, was responsible for identifying and securing properties for new Eat'n Park restaurants. As an architect, he also oversaw construction and renovation projects.

Always exploring locations as potential sites for new restaurants, Dave became aware of an interesting property in Somerset, about 70 miles southeast of Pittsburgh. The corner property was situated at a busy intersection, just off the Pennsylvania Turnpike. It had been owned by Robert Gilmour, whose company manufactured hoses, nozzles, and sprinklers, among other accessories. After his death, Mr. Gilmour's wife, Romaine, wanted to sell the property.

Many interested buyers recognized the potential of such a prime location and were willing to offer significant funds for the acquisition. Mrs. Gilmour was in a position to select from many suitors, including Eat'n Park.

Dave decided to pay a visit to Mrs. Gilmour and asked Jim Broadhurst to join him. "It was clear she had a great deal of respect for her late husband," Dave recalls. "Hearing her talk about him, Jim and I were both very moved, so we told her that, if she sold the property to us, we would erect a fountain as a memorial to her husband."

Mrs. Gilmour was so touched by the suggestion that she accepted Dave and Jim's offer. "Little did she know that Dave and I had no idea what it would take to build a large fountain on that busy intersection," Jim says, chuckling.

In August 1985, Eat'n Park purchased the 1.5-acre property. A year later, a new Eat'n Park restaurant opened on the site with a fountain positioned prominently across from the entrance, bearing a plaque paying tribute to Robert Gilmour.

Dave, who retired from Eat'n Park in 2005, looks at the transaction as one of the more satisfying of his career. "It was a really competitive process," he reflects. "Finding the way to make it happen was satisfying."

Mrs. Gilmour was overcome with emotion when the fountain was unveiled.

The fountain is a moving memorial to the late Mr. Gilmour, but in the past it occasionally created an unexpected issue. "When teenagers drove by the fountain, they would toss in boxes of laundry detergent," Jim explains. "We didn't anticipate seeing the intersection covered in bubbles."

A Passion for Learning

Education always has been of paramount importance to the leadership of Eat'n Park and, perhaps, to no one more than the late John Vichie.

When his father became ill, John dropped out of high school to get a job. It was 1950, and that job was parking cars at the first Eat'n Park restaurant on Saw Mill Run Boulevard. On John's first day on the job, his father died.

With his job now critically important to his family, John continued parking cars until the weather turned cold. He quickly realized that there were advantages to working inside the restaurant. When John stepped behind the grill as a cook, it was the beginning of a career that was centered around Eat'n Park food.

Carol Kijanka, executive assistant, Parkhurst Dining, remembers her late boss and friend, John Vichie.

Curious by nature, John was eager to learn to compensate for his lack of a high school diploma. He read all he could; he sought guidance from those around him; he went to trade shows; and he taught himself through trial and error. Eventually, John earned a General Education Diploma (GED).

"John knew a lot about a lot," remembers Carol Kijanka, who was John's executive assistant. "If he didn't know it, he would find the answer."

As he learned, John progressed in his career with Eat'n Park, moving from cook to positions that included restaurant manager, general manager, and district supervisor, overseeing a group of restaurants. His knowledge of Eat'n Park guests and of food ultimately earned him the position of director of product development in 1985. "It was a new, senior-level management position," Jim Broadhurst explains, "with the important responsibility of developing and testing new menu items."

John took that responsibility seriously and began looking for new products and new recipes that would work for operations in the kitchen and, at the same time, create exciting new menu items for guests.

"John was a great teacher and happy to share his knowledge and experience with anyone who asked. He had a larger-than-life personality, a great laugh, and was one of the smartest people I ever met," remembers Carol.

In 1997, John Vichie, beloved husband, father, colleague, friend, and 47-year team member of Eat'n Park, suffered a massive heart attack and died.

"When we think about John, we think of a man who demonstrated the importance of hard work, persistence, and personal integrity," Jim says. "The impact John had – introducing entrees that are still on our menu today, developing the bakery menu, and creating our soups – will be remembered as a stroke of genius."

To honor John's memory, Eat'n Park established the John Vichie Scholarship at Robert Morris University. The scholarship is awarded annually to a student or students pursuing a career in hospitality or business management.

"Education was very important to John; he had a passion for learning," Carol says. "And he loved this company."

Running a "Note-able" Operation

Chuck Sites began his career as a short-order cook at the South Park Eat'n Park restaurant on September 7, 1965. He ended his career as vice president of operations in 2006. In those 41 years, Chuck not only helped to shape the evolution of the restaurants, he also helped the people who worked for him to evolve.

"I believed in training my crew and giving them the right habits," Chuck says. "Minimize waste, maximize profits."

When Julius Ridgley was named manager at a Harrisburg Eat'n Park location, he reported to Chuck, who was a district supervisor at the time. "One of the things that Chuck was great at was coaching," Julius explains. "He was able to help you solve the problem on your own. And he almost never really made it about the business; it was more about you as an individual. He would just keep sticking those little Chuck-sized lessons in there, knowing that eventually they would take root."

Chuck Sites, former vice president of operations, created a standard for restaurant managers.

When Julius was beginning his next role as a general manager at the Dormont Eat'n Park, he eagerly awaited the first few operating statements, which were a measure of the restaurant's financial performance. He remembers his first three operating statements. The first two statements were "just OK." However, the third operating statement was the best Julius had ever seen. "I felt like my team and I had done a good job with our financials that month, but nobody said anything about it, so I didn't know," Julius remembers. "Maybe that was normal for everybody."

But one day when he arrived at the restaurant, he saw a letter in the mail from Chuck Sites who, by that point, no longer supervised Julius. "He sent me that operating statement, and he had written me a personal note and highlighted everything that was excellent on that statement," Julius explains. "He took the time out of his day to look into what I was doing and to let me know that I had done a really good job. He didn't have to do that. He could have completely ignored me for the rest of my career, but he let me know that I had done a good job and that he was happy with those results. That meant a lot."

Although Chuck retired in 2006, his lore continues. One example: 3" x 5" index cards.

Toward the conclusion of a restaurant visit, Chuck would walk the restaurant with the managers and show them what needed to be changed – where they had waste or what needed to be done better.

Julius Ridgley, manager of community and culture, appreciated the "Chuck-sized" lessons.

Chuck explains, "At the end of sessions, I'd hand the managers a 3x5 card, and I'd tell them to write the three things that were most important that I said that day. Never more than three. The managers and I loved the cards because they'd really pay attention."

Jim Bann, managing director of operations, Eat'n Park Restaurant Division, continues to utilize the index cards Chuck Sites introduced.

"Lo and behold, I have them right here," says Jim Bann, managing director of operations and a former restaurant manager, as he pulls index cards from his shirt pocket. "I write it all down so I don't forget those things. It's hard to remember everything, so you sure as heck want to make sure whenever you have an interaction again with that person that you remember something from that previous conversation. Index cards are one of those teaching things that Chuck was all about."

Whether it's through teaching moments or quiet praise, Chuck has left his mark on countless individuals.

Julius, who is now manager of community and culture with Eat'n Park Hospitality Group, says, "Every year that I'm alive, Chuck Sites gets smarter and smarter."

Cayman Islands

Williamsburg

River Walk in
San Antonio

4

A Traveling Show of Appreciation

In 1983, Kathy James went to Bermuda. "It was a Wednesday," she remembers, "when Jim Broadhurst asked me what I was doing that weekend. I didn't have plans – I was young and single. When I told him I wasn't doing anything, Jim asked, 'Do you want to go to Bermuda?'"

Jim explained that he and Suzy were thinking about a trip, and a travel-agent friend and his family were going to Bermuda. He hoped Kathy would join them. So, Kathy, all by herself, joined the travel agent and his family and headed for the pink-sand beaches.

The trip Suzy and Jim were thinking about, however, was not simply a getaway. The Broadhursts had been considering hosting an annual trip for Eat'n Park managers and their spouses or significant others, and Jim wanted Kathy to see if Bermuda would be an appropriate destination.

In 1984, the idea became a reality when the first managers' conference was held in Bermuda. Suzy, along with travel agent Sophea Chapas, planned every detail of that first trip, setting the standard for those that were to follow.

The trip was neither an incentive nor a reward, and all managers were included. The weekend was to include meetings – both informational and educational – team-building activities, special dinners, unique events, and amazing tours. The conference that began in 1984 continues today.

"It helps the spouse understand what the company is about, what the leadership is about, and just appreciate where you work," says JoAnn Walk, a district manager with the Restaurant Division. "It brings them into the company. It's something that really helps management stay around."

A key component of the trips is giving general managers access to otherwise behind-the-scenes activities that contribute to the host site's hospitality. In 1992, for example, on a trip to Williamsburg,

Virginia, Suzy arranged for the Eat'n Park entourage to tour the underground commissary that supports all Colonial Williamsburg restaurants. Few people know about the underground commissary, and even fewer have ever seen it.

"They make selections that have an educational piece to it," explains Dominic Fricioni, another district manager with the Restaurant Division. "When we went to Napa, for instance, they took us to vineyards. A sommelier gave us some really interesting education about wines that I wouldn't have gotten otherwise because Miller Lite® isn't a wine," he says with a laugh.

For Dominic Fricioni, a district manager with the Eat'n Park Restaurant Division, the general managers' conferences have refined his knowledge – and taste buds.

Suzy retired in 2014, and with her tutelage, Kathy James and Patty Shell, executive assistant to the chairman and executive assistant to the president and chief executive officer, respectively, gradually assumed responsibility for the general managers' conferences. Patty had assisted Suzy for years, and Kathy always had a role in the planning, making the duo Suzy's natural successors. Together, they scout destinations. "We have people come from 14 or 15 different geographic locations," Patty explains. "So, we need to look for destinations that people can easily access. It takes more than a year to plan each conference."

Suzy and Jim were hopeful when they began the tradition of company trips that it would expand the team members' experiences. In the early years of the trips, many of them had never been out of the Pittsburgh region, never been on an airplane, never stayed in a hotel, never spent time with other team members. "We are always pleased to see how the conferences widen team members' horizons, how they give them opportunities to see how others provide hospitality services," Suzy says. "The conferences enable them to develop friendships within the company, and they help to make them proud to be an Eat'n Park Hospitality Group team member. We like to think they contribute to the development of the culture of the company."

With Suzy Broadhurst's tutelage, Kathy James and Patty Shell now coordinate the general managers' conferences.

Miles of Memories

The general managers' conferences reinforce the family nature of the company culture. The Broadhurst family members and company executives are hosts, and the GMs' significant others are important participants. Typically, the highlight of the trip is an exclusive tour of a hospitality-related business.

But in 1994, the highlight of the trip was about commitment.

Jim Bann was a general manager at the Peach Street Eat'n Park, one of two Eat'n Park locations in Erie. The team members from both restaurants often gathered socially, sometimes playing volleyball on the beach or engaging in a friendly competition of softball.

One evening when Jim was out after work, he bumped into Richelle Spadacene, a server from the Erie State Street restaurant. A casual conversation led to dating, and after a year-long courtship, Jim Bann proposed to Richelle in October 1993.

A few months later at the company holiday party, Suzy and Jim Broadhurst congratulated the couple and asked about their wedding plans which, at that point, the engaged couple hadn't yet worked out. Jim Broadhurst immediately became the wedding planner.

"You know, we're going to San Antonio in a few months for the general managers' conference," he reminded the couple. "If you don't have any plans, we could put something together there." The groom-to-be remembers his reaction: "That's not going to happen! It's a GM trip!" But Jim Broadhurst insisted: "No, we can make this happen. This is part of the family, and it's a big part of what the company is."

On February 3, 1994, Jim Broadhurst and Richelle traveled by gondola along the River Walk in San Antonio to a little white church. Jim escorted Richelle from the gondola down the aisle as a mariachi band that Suzy hired was playing in the background. Eat'n Park team members – including Jim Bann's two brothers who worked for the company – and spouses were seated in a scenic garden, smiling as Jim Bann watched his bride approaching. The nearby old convent served as the reception site for the celebration that followed the ceremony.

Nearly three decades and two daughters later, the groom sums it up: "It was pretty awesome!"

In 1992, the general managers' conference was in Williamsburg, Virginia. At the time, Dennis Quinlisk was the general manager at the Whitehall Eat'n Park restaurant.

"On the general managers' trips, Suzy always commissioned a gold charm from where the trip was held," Dennis explains. "My wife put it on her necklace, but it fell off during the trip. The last day of the trip, I ran to every jewelry shop in Williamsburg, but I could not find the charm. I went up to Suzy as we were getting on the bus to leave. I said, 'Suzy, I still got a little bit of time. Linda lost her charm. I'm trying to get her another one because she's heartbroken. Where did you buy that?' Suzy takes her necklace off, takes the charm off, and gives it to me."

"We are always pleased to see how the conferences widen team members' horizons, how they give them opportunities to see how others provide hospitality services."

— Suzy Broadhurst

5

Diversifying for the Future

For Eat'n Park Restaurants, the 1980s were a great decade. Additional restaurants had been built, sales were picking up, and the company had moved outside its heritage market of southwestern Pennsylvania.

The leadership of the company was talented and believed they had the capacity to do more. They wanted to build on the strength of the restaurants, possibly through acquisitions.

It was the early 1990s when Jim, along with Dan Wilson, then the vice president of corporate planning and development, began considering how the company could accelerate growth beyond simply adding a few restaurants each year.

The diversification required adding highly trained chefs to the team.

"Competition in the family-restaurant sector was intensifying, and we preferred to broaden the company's financial risk and then pursue a wider national footprint," Jim explains. They needed a mechanism to evaluate possible growth opportunities, so they developed five criteria for diversification:

Criteria for Diversification

1) **Pursue an opportunity in food service where the company could again become one of the best in the category without competing with the existing Eat'n Park restaurant operations**

2) **Choose a business that did not require a large investment in facilities**

3) **Build on strength as a regional player**

4) **Leverage existing support services at Eat'n Park**

5) **Create advancement opportunities for team members**

With input from Bob Moore, past president – who by then had retired but remained active on the Board of Directors – the team concluded they would go with their strength and leverage existing resources. They identified four possible paths.

One option was to develop a new restaurant concept. If they pursued that, the construction cost – at that time, about $2 million per restaurant – would limit how much growth the company could sustain.

Franchising Eat'n Park restaurants had been an option for a long time. "We never looked at it seriously," Jim explains. "Our menu is complex, and once you get into the franchising business, it's tough to maintain consistency throughout the chain."

A third option was to purchase an existing restaurant concept. In the mid-1990s, PNC – Eat'n Park's bank – approached the company with an opportunity to invest in Hacienda Restaurants, a Mexican restaurant chain in the state of Indiana. "PNC was interested in investing in the restaurant segment," Dan Wilson explains. "They had approval, but only if they had an operator who would invest with them."

Dan traveled to Indiana to take a closer look at the opportunity and was satisfied with what he learned. "The purchase agreement we put together provided that Eat'n Park would have franchise rights for that concept in our footprint with no royalty fee," Dan explains.

Although they were not interested immediately in building Hacienda restaurants in western Pennsylvania, they liked having that option. "At the very least," Dan says, "it would be a good investment, we would learn something, and we'd have a seat on the Board of Directors."

In October 1995, the Board of Directors of Eat'n Park authorized a $1 million investment in Hacienda Restaurants, Inc. Other than Eat'n Park holding a seat on the restaurant's board, the company never did anything with the investment and eventually sold their share of the company. Instead, they focused their attention on a different possibility.

The team evaluating growth opportunities determined the final option was the best: operate someone else's investment and contract with them to take it to the next level. Entering the non-commercial food service segment would require a smaller investment (no longer always the case), and it would create the opportunity for the company to leverage its reputation in order to attract business to the new entity.

"That really brought it down to focusing on contract dining," Jim remembers. "Because there was not a big capital requirement to put money into new construction, we felt that while we developed the contract dining business we could continue to grow Eat'n Park and invest in remodeling restaurants. We didn't want to do anything that would jeopardize growth and success for our team members."

How do you begin to build a company that will provide a service you've never offered? You fortuitously cross paths with someone who has expertise in the new service line. Enter Mitch Possinger.

An Intersection of Introductions

Mitch Possinger had recently resigned from working for the Wood Company, a contract dining service company in Allentown, Pennsylvania. He was in the early stages of developing a business plan for a new contract dining business of his own. Cura Hospitality would be dedicated exclusively to long-term care facilities.

At the Wood Company, Mitch had a colleague – Will Chizmar – who was a graduate of The Pennsylvania State University School of Hospitality Management. Will and the senior leaders at Eat'n Park had crossed paths through a shared connection with the school. When the concept of diversification was becoming a possibility, Dan Wilson reached out to Will. And just as Mitch was beginning to fine tune his business plan for Cura Hospitality in Allentown, Will introduced him to Dan.

The year was 1995, and Jim and Dan decided to bring Mitch on as a consultant to help develop the new contract dining business. He had the perfect background to help them identify opportunities to explore.

"I was engaged in the fall of 1995 to work with Dan to do a market assessment, kind of a feasibility study," Mitch recalls. "Could there be an opportunity for Eat'n Park to do something on the non-commercial side of contract services? So, we did a strategic plan for the board. We looked at all the segments – K-12, higher education, corporate, and healthcare."

The contract dining business was – and still is – dominated by a few national players. As huge corporations, they tend to focus on larger clients where there is opportunity for a greater return on investment.

"We knew about the big players, but we didn't see many companies at a smaller level," Jim says. "They seemed to come and go pretty quickly. So, we thought we might have an interest in a boutique-type business."

The team casually reached out to some contacts, including their bank, to gauge the receptivity to the concept of Eat'n Park introducing a contract dining division. "Would it be accepted in the marketplace, run by a family dining restaurant chain? That was the question we were trying to get answered," Dan says. "It became clear we would need to set this thing up on its own."

The path to diversification was beginning to take shape. There would be a separate company that would provide contract dining services to smaller private colleges and universities. As the team considered their focus, corporate dining and special venues – like museums – began to emerge as other areas where the new company could distinguish itself.

Questionable Timing

With planning taking place behind the scenes, Jim was surprised one day by a phone call from Neil Binstock who was running dining services at Carnegie Mellon University at the time. It was mid-November, and the university's food service provider just informed Neil that they were pulling out of their contract at the conclusion of the term. Neil was facing the prospect of hungry students returning in January and having no way to feed them. He had heard that Eat'n Park was considering entering the contract dining arena.

Neil's call to Jim was to ask if there was any way – on a short-term basis – Eat'n Park could step in and help with providing food service to Carnegie Mellon, beginning in about six weeks. The university would eventually run the service, but they needed a short-term fix.

"They needed somebody to come in and provide management oversight, but they wanted to run it themselves," Mitch explains. "They were looking for sort of a hybrid relationship."

So, was this the worst possible timing or the greatest opportunity? It depends on who you ask.

"This was really kind of premature because we didn't even have the business plan approved by the board yet," Mitch remembers saying. "We had no resources at all."

Mitch Possinger played a strong role in launching Parkhurst Dining.

Jim had a different point of view. "It was perfect for us," he says. "We got our feet wet. We knew if we gained some experience, it would be even easier to call on our first potential client."

Mitch recruited a former colleague to lead the Carnegie Mellon effort. Dave Connelly had run food service operations for major state universities throughout Pennsylvania. Mitch recalls the conversation with Dave: "I said, 'How about if we hire you on an independent-contractor basis? Give me a three-month guarantee. This is what I'll pay you, and if you find a permanent opportunity that you think is better, just give me a month's notice.'"

The Contract Dining Division of Eat'n Park was officially launched in January 1996 through a signed agreement with Carnegie Mellon University and with Dave Connelly directing the operation and Dan Wilson serving as president.

Once they gained board approval of the contract dining business plan, Jim, Dan, and Mitch began to move forward quickly. Contract dining wouldn't require a huge financial investment. That left just two small things the team needed: staff and clients.

The path to diversification was beginning to take shape. There would be a separate company that would provide contract dining services to smaller private colleges and universities. As the team considered their focus, corporate dining and special venues – like museums – began to emerge as other areas where the new company could distinguish itself.

Building the Base

Addressing the staffing need required someone who had culinary training and knew food, someone who could knock on doors and secure business, and someone who knew how to run the operations of a contract dining business.

Mitch knew the perfect person.

Nick Camody was a former colleague of Mitch's at the Wood Company. He had a culinary background, and his responsibilities included operations and sales. Mitch contacted him about the opportunity with this new company.

"I certainly wasn't looking to move to Pittsburgh," Nick says with a chuckle. "I was from the other side of the state, and my wife grew up in New England. Philadelphia? Maybe. Mid-Atlantic? Probably. But Pittsburgh? How would I explain that to my wife?"

Nick agreed to a meeting with Jim, Dan, and Mitch. He was intrigued by the concept they were describing. It would be an opportunity to use both his culinary skills and his operations experience. And, Nick realized, they were right – there really wasn't a strong player in the small-to-mid-size college and university market.

"I really enjoyed the idea of starting something new and being part of forming the company," Nick says. "How were we going to do it? What were we going to do? What type of business were we going to look at?"

But if Nick were to commit to this concept, he wanted a commitment in return: if he were to join the team and if they wanted to succeed, they needed to build a brand around a set of principles and standards.

"I really enjoyed the idea of starting something new and being part of forming the company."

— Nick Camody

"Jim wanted to make sure we delivered what we said, and that was very important to me, as well," explains Nick. "In our business, reputation is everything. And Jim was open to that – he really wanted quality versus quantity."

It was January 1996, and Mr. and Mrs. Camody started packing.

What's in a Name?

Once Nick was on board, he made a confession – he hated the name Contract Dining Division of Eat'n Park.

"We wanted the connection with Eat'n Park," Nick explains. "I can't recall who came up with the name," Mitch adds, "but someone had the idea that, since this was the first creation within Eat'n Park that really had Jim Broadhurst's fingerprints on it, the name should reflect the old and the new."

"'Park' sounded a little upscale," Nick explains, "and 'hurst,' of course, comes from Jim's last name. So, we put those together, and it sounded really good."

The team at Highmark, Parkhurst's first corporate client

Following on the heels of the Carnegie Mellon engagement, the unanticipated opportunities continued when a request for proposals (RFP) arrived at Eat'n Park's office. "The first day I showed up here in January, St. Vincent College's RFP was in the mail," Nick remembers. "I mean, it just showed up. They heard we were getting into the contract dining business."

Nick and his new colleagues responded to the RFP and won the contract. Effective July 1, 1996, Parkhurst Dining had its first signed client. And more quickly followed.

Carnegie Mellon transitioned from a signed agreement to get the university through a transition to a signed contract, effective July 15, 1996. The first corporate account, Highmark, was signed the last weekend of December 1996, and Parkhurst had the account up and running on January 2, 1997. "We had three really good contracts," Nick recalls, "in less than a year."

Building the Family

As Nick became more involved with the culinary and operational sides of the business, Parkhurst still needed someone to lead sales. To fill that need, Jim looked to Chicago to try to persuade a familiar face to join the team – Jeff Broadhurst.

Jeff, the eldest of the three Broadhurst sons, had earned his MBA and was working as a wholesaler of mutual funds with Federated Investors (now Federated Hermes), an investment management firm headquartered in Pittsburgh. After three years in Louisville, Jeff was in his third year with Federated's Chicago office, with a successful sales career well underway.

"It was an incredible company – still is," Jeff says. "I loved it. I had great clients and the best boss ever, Jim Hamilton. Things were pretty good for me in Chicago. I had a boat on Lake Michigan, and I'd call clients from the boat. It was a nice, relaxed, calm atmosphere."

It was an incoming call that rocked Jeff's boat.

"I called Jeff to see if he would be interested in coming back to Pittsburgh to work in sales for Parkhurst," Jim says. "Sales was something he was always interested in and good at. When he answered my call, he was on his boat. That made me think that I might have an uphill battle!"

Jim succeeded in convincing Jeff that the opportunity to lead the development of a brand-new company far outweighed boating on Lake Michigan. By April of 1996, Jeff was back in Pittsburgh and onboard, navigating new waters as he began to build a sales program for Parkhurst.

Which meant, in essence, selling something that didn't exist.

"Starting a contract dining business gave us the opportunity to think through what wasn't available in the marketplace," Jeff says. "We'd listen to what the client wanted and say, 'Sure, we can do that.' Then we'd go back and figure out how we were going to do it. We were creating things completely around what the client wanted."

Jeff and his colleagues knew there were two things that always would be key ingredients in delivering what the client wanted: very high-quality food made from scratch and very good service.

Jeff, Jim, Dan, Nick, and Mitch developed foundational pillars for Parkhurst; they became the basis for the Parkhurst brand. Over the years, Parkhurst added to the original pillars, and the values continue to guide the company today.

Parkhurst Foundational Pillars
- **Culinary Gold Standards**
- **We Care About Our Team Members**
- **Genuine Client Relationships**
- **Responsible Sourcing Philosophy**

As Jeff developed the sales process, Parkhurst was responding to more RFPs and receiving more invitations to meet with potential clients' selection committees. Jim, Dan, Jeff, Mitch, and Nick attended each new business meeting, either in total or some combination of the team. "We wanted to demonstrate that the highest-level executives were looking after Parkhurst," Jim explains. "Our presence sent a message: when things went well, we would be there with the client to celebrate; and when things weren't running as desired, we would be there with the client to resolve the issue."

With 50 years of history, Eat'n Park had a reputation that the team believed would help them to secure clients, particularly in the local market. "Many people believed that, since we were successful with Eat'n Park, they could trust us to make contract food service work for them," Jim recalls.

"They trusted what we told them, given our reputation in the community," Jeff adds. "That helped us – we could get a meeting, they understood who we are, they trusted us, and respected the organization."

~~~~~~

With 50 years of history, Eat'n Park had a reputation that the team believed would help them to secure clients, particularly in the local market.

~~~~~~

But in those early years, Nick discovered that not everyone was thrilled with the Eat'n Park connection. "The people that were in this region only knew Eat'n Park from Eat'n Park restaurants, and they loved Eat'n Park restaurants. But they didn't see the connection," Nick remembers. "We kept getting questions: 'How are you going to translate that to what we do? How are you going to serve our Board of Trustees? And how are you going to have waitstaff that can serve wine?' So, we had to do a lot of training around that. And we really had to build our brand fast."

"We had to prove it to everybody. We'd say, 'Oh, yeah, we can do that,' but they wanted to see it, and we were a little out of luck at the time because we had nothing to show," Nick remembers. "We'd ask for a presentation we could bring food to. We'd prepare the food and serve it, which wasn't common at the time. Every time we did a presentation, the client selection team knew that we had the wherewithal to do it. It was really well worth the effort."

As the client base began to develop, the small team started to assemble a recipe file. "We were the taste testers," Nick laughs. "We kept trying new things, new ideas, new recipes."

Eventually, they formed a Culinary Council, a group of Parkhurst executive chefs who developed new concepts. "We wanted to be authentic, so we created recipes around that authenticity. And we brought in people from the industry – Culinary Institute of America instructors and cookbook authors."

FORE-Ward Progress

In the mid-1990s, four graduates of Carnegie Mellon University founded FORE Systems and chose Pittsburgh as the headquarters for the new company. Makers of computer hardware, FORE Systems grew rapidly and quickly became a formidable player in the global marketplace. Rapid growth necessitated a much larger headquarters, and the company built a campus in Warrendale, a suburb north of Pittsburgh. The founders hired Bill Bates, an architect, to manage the design and construction of the new campus, including the employee cafeteria.

Bill Bates introduced Parkhurst Dining to FORE Systems.

As Bill got started with his new role, he issued a request for proposals (RFP) for food service equipment, installers, and contractors. "One of the bidders was Joe Bryan who was president of Brysco Food Service," Bill remembers. "I didn't know it at the time, but Brysco was a part of Eat'n Park."

Joe Bryan was married to Jim Broadhurst's younger sister, Beth (who passed away in 1995). Joe asked Bill to consider a turnkey development for the FORE cafeteria. Joe explained that rather than having a generic cafeteria, another division of Eat'n Park – Parkhurst Dining – could work with Brysco in the design process, and then Parkhurst would run the cafeteria.

"On the surface, that sounds intriguing," Bill remembers saying, "but the orders that I've gotten from the four founders of the company were that this dining facility is supposed to be commensurate with the competition that they were vying with to hire employees – companies from Silicon Valley and Seattle."

Bill had done his research and knew that the big tech companies were using large food service providers whose approach to corporate dining was, in his opinion, cookie cutter. He believed that Parkhurst could provide something different, but the company had nothing to show because it had never done anything similar to the FORE project.

"I went to the founders and said, 'These guys are interested in the business,'" Bill remembers. "And they said, 'Don't bother us with this. We don't want an Eat'n Park. We've got to compete for these top-notch engineers coming from California and Boston, so we need the best.'"

Not willing to take 'no' for an answer – and since they couldn't take FORE to Parkhurst – Nick Camody and Dan Wilson offered to take Parkhurst to FORE. The FORE founders were very reluctant to accept the offer, but Bill convinced them. He also counseled Nick: "Whatever you do, don't mention Eat'n Park. The founders all said they don't want Eat'n Park food."

With their own equipment set up in a conference room, Nick and a colleague served lunch to the founders and Bill. FORE invited the team back, and they provided another delicious meal with an entirely different menu.

The founders were impressed by Parkhurst, but one of the them had a question: "Where's the Eat'n Park salad bar? I want the salad bar."

Once they were given the go ahead, Parkhurst and Brysco collaborated to design the new cafeteria. "They redesigned the kitchen from what the original spec was so that it suited what they anticipated they would need," Bill explains. "They interviewed the employees before they started and asked them what they were interested in having for meals, and that drove the design of the kitchen and the menu."

The corporate dining world Parkhurst was entering at FORE was anything but traditional. "It was unlike anything that a caterer would've typically been required to do on a corporate campus," Bill explains. "And by that, I mean there was a culture where every employee had ownership and could tell the CEO what they wanted in the cafeteria."

Bryan Marince was managing the operation at the time, and he had an idea: What if FORE employees would share family recipes? "We wanted to make the dining experience personal," Bryan says, explaining his strategy. The result was enthusiastic.

"We received recipes for chilis, soups, barbeques," he says. "And we always credited the employee who provided the recipe. It created great conversations. People were refreshing their minds, not constantly thinking about work – and that was a goal of the owners."

The service Parkhurst expected to provide quickly expanded. FORE had a large international employee population, so Bryan and his team were testing their skills with Asian and Indian food. Many employees worked long hours, so Parkhurst accommodated different schedules. When the founders asked for a way to get people out of their offices, Parkhurst responded with carnivals, wine tastings, and massages – all arranged by Bryan.

"They bent over backwards to do things like that," Bill Bates says. "And they earned a reputation as being the best restaurant in town."

The greatest satisfaction may have come when someone from a large Silicon Valley competitor visited FORE. "He was so jealous," Bill says. "He thought our food was so much better than his."

Bryan Marince, director of corporate dining, Parkhurst Dining

Eventually, the founders sold FORE to a British company. Shortly after the sale, Bill received a call from Jeff Broadhurst asking him if he would be interested in having lunch with Jim Broadhurst. "That's when Jim told me they needed a vice president of real estate. That led to 16 years with Eat'n Park," Bill says.

After he was on board at Eat'n Park for a while, Bill Bates shared a personal detail with the Broadhursts: his wife, Maggie, is the niece of Larry Hatch!

Square Peg, Round Hole

Things were moving quickly, and behind the scenes, the fledgling company was scrambling to put systems in place.

"Parkhurst is coming in from scratch, a start up," explains Bryan Marince, director of corporate dining. "No structure at all, other than the vision of Nick Camody and the leadership team." Bryan was one of the first employees hired. He had a strong restaurant background, which was exactly what Nick was looking for. But contract dining requests for proposals – the proposals themselves – were new concepts for Bryan. Proposals were a big process, especially because Parkhurst would be bidding against larger companies with years of experience.

"I remember on a Friday night we were putting a proposal together," Bryan says. "We had one printer. There were three, four, maybe five of us putting a proposal together for a corporate account. The printer was too slow, so I took the files home. Go home, print stuff, come back, put the proposal together. We got the account."

While most team members at the Corporate Support Center stayed focused on Eat'n Park Restaurants, a core of senior staff was developing the necessary systems and procedures for the new company.

Carol Kijanka, a long-time Eat'n Park team member, began working with Parkhurst when it was in the concept stage, providing support to the team in every way possible. Now the executive assistant at Parkhurst, she witnessed a transition that was, at times, less than easy. "People understood diversification, but there was a learning curve," Carol remembers. "The restaurants belonged to us; but we didn't own these Parkhurst accounts."

The differences between the restaurants and contract dining touched just about every part of the business. "Every client has something unique from a financial perspective," explains Julie Brochetti, vice president, accounting and controller. "We had to learn about new clients and what was important to them."

Julie joined Parkhurst in its early stages. "We were very Excel based then, and we would dial into the sites every week and pull the financial information, site by site," she says. "That was fine when we had 20 accounts, but as Parkhurst grew, it became clear that we had a lot of opportunities to systemize some things, to automate things."

To further complicate things, there was a new guy in town. "We brought Nick in from the outside – that wasn't the Eat'n Park way," Carol explains. "We promote from within. Everything about Parkhurst was so different from what we were used to, and people weren't necessarily helpful to him."

"It was a struggle for a lot of people in the organization at first," Brooks Broadhurst explains. The middle of the three Broadhurst brothers, Brooks joined Eat'n Park in the mid-1990s, and purchasing was among his responsibilities.

He first dipped his hands into the Eat'n Park business when he was in high school and worked as a dishwasher at the South Hill Village restaurant. He moved to pursue a degree in hotel/restaurant management at Penn State and applied his dishwashing skills at the State College Eat'n Park. "They never promoted me, so I left," Brooks jokes.

When he graduated from college, Brooks accepted an opportunity to manage Mike's American Grill, a popular restaurant in the Washington, D.C., area known for the quality of its food and service. After a couple of years of long hours and loud bars, Brooks was ready when his father asked him to return to Pittsburgh to take on a new challenge at the company.

Eat'n Park's Distribution Center is the hub for restaurant inventory. It's an operation that requires managing what comes in, what goes out, and where it goes. With the growth of the company, however, the inventory was too large to be managed manually, so Jim Broadhurst wanted Brooks to develop an automated inventory system for the Distribution Center. First, Brooks needed to complete the company's management training program, which he did at the Edgewood restaurant.

"I implemented a new purchasing and inventory system," Brooks explains. "I worked for Ron Champe when I completed the management training program. He was vice president of purchasing and may have been the first person to hold that role. He was a great mentor when I came into the office. He was meticulous in everything he did…from understanding our business to rehabbing old Chevy Corvettes." Brooks remembers one instance, in particular: "One time he came in with blisters on the tips of his fingers from buffing bolts all night so they would shine on the bottom of his car! He was tenacious and taught me a lot – not only about purchasing!"

~~~~~~

"I implemented a new purchasing and inventory system," Brooks explains. "I worked for Ron Champe … he was a great mentor."

~~~~~~

Eventually, Brooks took over management of the Distribution Center, and when Parkhurst was taking shape, Brooks developed the purchasing systems for the new company. But Parkhurst wasn't simply a new company, it was a very different company.

"We were Eat'n Park Restaurants. We had a way we did things   this is how we train people, this is how we buy things, this is how we serve things, these are the systems we use," Brooks explains. "And that completely had to get blown up because, while we were still selling food, it was in a completely different way."

Clearly, there was a lot of juggling in the beginning. "Everything at the Corporate Support Center was set up for a restaurant," explains Bill Jones, director of catering for Parkhurst client PNC. "At Parkhurst, we think differently. We're client driven, so whatever the client wants, we relay to the corporate division. It's about quality, and it's about making clients happy and using whatever vendor it takes to do that."

It quickly became clear to the leadership team that operating Parkhurst required a complete culture shift from operating Eat'n Park restaurants. As a family restaurant, Eat'n Park never served liquor; now, Parkhurst needed a liquor license. "Where do we buy the liquor? How do we run a liquor license? Where's the liability?" Bill remembers wondering. "It was a whole new thought process."

Today, when Nick Camody thinks about the challenges in the early days, he laughs. He remembers one call in particular from Dave Wohleber, then chief financial officer. "He calls me one day and says, 'I don't know what your people are doing; they're nuts. Somebody went out and bought a torch. Why would you need a torch?' I told him we needed it for crème brulee. Dave says, 'What the heck is crème brulee?'" It was a steep learning curve.

Nick Camody needed to educate his colleagues about new aspects of hospitality.

One of Parkhurst's corporate clients held board retreats at the CEO's vacation home at Deep Creek Lake. "He was British," Nick explains, "so he wouldn't drink a port less than 20 years old, and he insisted on the best cigars we could find. Our chef used to fly down to Deep Creek with them and cook all the meals and stay at the house."

It was time for another phone call from Dave Wohleber.

"Dave was worked up," Nick relates. "And he says, 'You know your people are buying cigars and port? What are they doing that for?' I told him it was for the CEO of a client, and that's what he likes. After a pause, Dave says, 'Well, can you save a cigar for me?' It was crazy. It was such a different business line, and nobody understood that we needed all those things."

A Fast Start

By the end of Parkhurst's third year of operation, there were five accounts. "Normally, when you have a start-up, you get really small accounts because you don't have a reputation around a big account," Jeff Broadhurst explains. "We were fortunate enough to get some larger accounts."

One larger account that was considering Parkhurst invited the team to do a presentation at their Atlanta office. "We flew down, rented a car, put the menu together, and spent a couple grand at Whole Foods," Bryan Marince remembers. "I went to a Marriott and got hotel rooms with kitchenettes. Five different chefs, making five different items, in five different hotel rooms with little kitchens – there was no hurdle we didn't collectively sit down as a team and say, 'How do we overcome it?'"

Parkhurst won the account.

Up Close and Personalized

"It was an interesting start, but the market was ready for something different, and we offered something different," Nick Camody explains. "We called it, 'Kitchen Forward,' where our goal was to knock down the wall of the kitchen and prepare foods in front of people. It was an approach used by some restaurants, but it wasn't happening in contract dining at the time. We wanted to do it with fresh food because we were doing it in front of guests, so we couldn't be taking frozen stuff out of a bag and saying we were preparing fresh food. We went in with a chef-driven, Kitchen Forward concept, and we put everything out in front of the guest and cooked it to order. It forced us to go in a direction that was beneficial for Parkhurst. We were leaders; we were out in the forefront."

Nick Camody knew exactly how to impress tennis legend Billie Jean King – racquet-shaped pasta.

What a Serve!

When Parkhurst made a new business pitch to Cedar Crest College in Allentown in 2002, the team was a bit startled by the selection committee's response: Start immediately.

The setting was familiar to Nick Camody – he started his career at Cedar Crest as a dishwasher. He was returning now, prepared to stay a week or two, to oversee the team setting up the account.

The new Parkhurst team's first meal was a fundraising dinner for Cedar Crest. The guest of honor was tennis legend Billie Jean King.

"The college wanted a pasta course," Nick remembers. "I didn't want to have something like spaghetti; we wanted to make sure that whatever we served, she could eat without getting messy."

So, Nick paid a visit to Pittsburgh's famed Pennsylvania Macaroni Company to purchase just the right pasta: Racchette #90 – macaroni in the shape of tennis racquets.

"When we brought those out and served them to Billie Jean, she went crazy. She couldn't believe it."

New Beginnings

In Latin, cura means: care of the soul; to attend to the body with food. As Parkhurst was taking shape, Mitch Possinger was still trying to nourish the finances of Cura Hospitality, his Allentown-based company.

"I was scrambling to try to raise money to start Cura," Mitch recalls. "We got our first client in April of 1996 while I was doing the fundraising," he explains. "We had two or three clients that were cobbled together with my own personal cash to just get it going until I could raise the bigger amount of capital."

cura®
HOSPITALITY
Enhancing Life Around Great Food sm

Mitch stopped himself from hoping that Eat'n Park might be interested in investing in Cura, knowing that Eat'n Park had decided to begin the Parkhurst venture. "The divine intervention part of the story is that my wife, Jamie, and I were in New York City at Christmastime for a day," Mitch recalls. "And, of course, Times Square, Park Avenue, Fifth Avenue, it's jammed with people. You can hardly walk on the sidewalks. To get off the street, we go into the Williams-Sonoma store, which is packed. I walk around the corner of this huge, completely tourist-packed store, and I run into Jim Broadhurst."

Both were equally surprised to see the other. After sharing some light conversation, Jim asked why Mitch hadn't sent him a copy of the Cura business plan. Mitch recounts, "I said, 'Well, I wasn't sure you were interested. It seemed like you had so much going on.'"

Once Jim and his team evaluated Mitch's business plan, Eat'n Park became an investor in Cura. Three years after the launch of Parkhurst, Eat'n Park Hospitality Group purchased the remainder of Cura Hospitality stock, becoming the sole owner.

A Bold Prediction

The purchase of Cura fit with Jim's interest in diversification, and Cura was another contract food business, so it fit with Parkhurst.

However, the path didn't appear as clear cut to everyone. In 1999, Eat'n Park was celebrating its 50th anniversary, and to commemorate the milestone, the general managers' conference that January was in Grand Cayman Island.

It was at a meeting on that trip when Jim introduced Mitch to the company and announced that Eat'n Park would be acquiring Cura Hospitality. "We had college accounts, we had corporate accounts," Jim remembers, "and now we were going to provide hospitality services to long-term care facilities. It would be the third arm of contract dining."

When Jim made the announcement, he also made a stunning prediction. "I know you people aren't going to believe this," he said to the group, "but I really think that the combination of Parkhurst and this new venture, Cura Hospitality, will someday equal or exceed the volume of business that we're doing at Eat'n Park."

No doubt, some people in the room believed Jim had spent too much time in the hot island sun.

Publicly and privately, people may have been questioning the wisdom of what seemed to be a rapid diversification. But Jim, Dan, Jeff, Mitch, and Nick had a plan, and they were working it. With Mitch again in Allentown, the home base of Cura, Parkhurst had a presence in both the western and eastern halves of the state.

The strategy for Parkhurst involved growing the client base in concentric circles. Begin in Allegheny County, where Eat'n Park's reputation was solid and the Broadhurst name was known. Concurrently, begin in Lehigh County where Mitch and Cura were well-respected.

Gradually, the company expanded to the next circle – counties surrounding Allegheny and surrounding Lehigh. And so, the growth of the contract food service company accelerated.

Of course, there were challenges in the early days, but the path continued to evolve for the growing company.

Expansion into new geographic markets was done with great caution. The team wanted to ensure they were delivering what they promised – hiring the right team members and, as a result, creating relationships with clients.

"We wanted to move slowly because we wanted to make sure we were doing our jobs," says Nick. "Jim really believed in that, and we believed in it because we thought that would enable us to really do a quality job and create real relationships with those clients."

"I really think that the combination of Parkhurst and this new venture, Cura Hospitality, will someday equal or exceed the volume of business that we're doing at Eat'n Park."

— Jim Broadhurst

An Amicable Parting

Cura was an integral part of Eat'n Park Hospitality Group for 16 years. But by 2013, the long-term care industry was beginning to change. And Cura needed to change with it.

Long-term care facilities were beginning to follow the lead of their healthcare counterparts, with several being merged into larger entities. "Our clients were consolidating," Mitch explains. "We were a boutique player, so we had a disadvantage with purchasing power. Personal relationships, old-fashioned values, and highly customizable service were always our focus."

In 2015, Elior Group, a global corporation and industry leader in the provision of contract catering, concession catering, and support services, approached Eat'n Park Hospitality Group. They knew Cura Hospitality was a strong brand, and they were interested in acquiring it. The sale enabled the Hospitality Group to accelerate growth in Parkhurst's corporate and education segments.

"Mitch Possinger was a great asset to our company and a good friend," Jim reflects. "We had a special relationship, and I didn't want to lose him, but the changes in the marketplace made the sale the correct decision."

Mark Broadhurst joined the company in 2003 to develop new concepts. Today, he is the chief operating officer of Parkhurst Dining.

Elbow Grease

Nick Camody remembers, "We hit a stride where our reputation was growing beyond our region. We were starting to receive RFPs from places that we weren't thinking of at the time, but we ended up thinking about them quickly because they were great locations."

The spread of Parkhurst's reputation was largely the result of the company's culture: an emphasis on high-quality food, extreme attention to detail and – when it comes to clients and guests – a do-whatever-it-takes attitude.

Bryan Marince remembers seeing that attitude in action when Parkhurst was taking over the Robert Morris University account. The team was scheduled to gain access at 8:00 on a Friday night, but the outgoing provider was slow moving out, and Parkhurst wasn't granted access until well after midnight.

"We were sitting on a grassy knoll waiting to get in," Bryan recalls. "It was me, Nick Camody, Jeff Broadhurst, and about five other people. As soon as we got permission to go in, we saw that a great deal of work needed to be done to get the space up to Parkhurst standards. Jeff Broadhurst got up underneath the hood of the grill – the dirtiest part of the job – and he was scrubbing. We were blown away that Jeff would do that. That set the culture."

Growing a Concept

Mark Broadhurst, the youngest of the sons, joined the company in 2003 to develop new concepts. In 2012, he also joined the Parkhurst team as vice president, corporate dining and retail development, eventually rising to his current role as chief operating officer of Parkhurst Dining.

"At Parkhurst we create new concepts every day," Mark explains. "We're creating a whole new concept from scratch, so we're always looking at something new and reinventing ourselves."

With the higher-ed business well underway, Mark focused on growing the corporate side of the contract dining business. Parkhurst had secured some corporate accounts, but always by responding to requests for proposals, never initiating the process. "We needed to take a more proactive approach," Mark says. "We were doing a good job, but now it was time to go out and tell our story."

As Mark and his colleagues made new contacts and spent more time in the field, they made a pleasant discovery. "It was an interesting time in corporate dining. A lot of people were starting to realize that having a great food program is a value to their employees. The newer startups and tech companies saw this as a really great way to recruit people."

There was a second discovery: today's college students are tomorrow's corporate employees. "Sooner or later, as people retire in corporate dining, they're replaced by new people coming out of college, and those needs come into the corporate dining world," explains Chris Fitz, a Parkhurst district manager. "If we don't stay on pulse with the college environment, we fail in the corporate environment."

Culture Crosses Miles

As the geographic footprint of Parkhurst expands, the company's culture needs to be infused into new geographic areas, carried out by new team members who have likely never heard of Parkhurst or Eat'n Park. How does that culture travel over the miles?

"A lot of it comes from promoting from within," Chris Fitz explains. "One of the biggest successes is when we have somebody who has worked for us and they relocate to a different community, different territory, and they're able to bring that culture and start it from the top down."

"We start well ahead of time to infuse our culture," Bryan Marince adds. "When we open a Chicago location, for example, we offer people in Pittsburgh the opportunity to work it. We try to open with a Parkhurst person who has been with the company, transferring them from Pittsburgh. Now, we build strength in Chicago so that when we open our next client site in that area, we have a team that can take our culture to the new client site."

Managers from all Parkhurst locations frequently return to Pittsburgh for ongoing training. And district managers travel to client sites and get to know the new staff. "I might have dinner with a new manager and his family," Bryan says. "We get to know each other. We're not just a corporate company. There are faces, there are personalities. And that's what the Broadhurst family did a great job infusing."

Staying in Tune with Client Needs

As Parkhurst grew, the company's reputation did, too. It didn't take long for requests for the company's catering services to multiply. Many of the requests were traditional, including private dinners for college presidents and corporate events. But some were unexpected. Among the opportunities, Parkhurst catered the G-20 Summit held in Pittsburgh in 2009, catered the Republican Senators' Luncheon in the U.S. Capitol Building four times, provided food services for the U.S. Open at the famed Oakmont Country Club, and provides meals for visiting Major League Baseball teams at PNC Park.

And in 2016, requests hit a high note.

Willie Nelson, Neil Young, and John Mellencamp had organized a concert – Farm Aid – to raise awareness and funding for endangered family farms. The first concert was held on September 22, 1985, in Champaign, Illinois. Farm Aid is held annually, and locally grown, farm-fresh food is served at each concert.

Bryan Marince received a memorable phone call from the organizers of the Farm Aid concerts. This is his story:

"Farm Aid came into Burgettstown to Key Bank Pavilion (now the Pavilion at Star Lake) in 2016. It was a nightmare for them to get the food for their groups, so someone suggested Parkhurst. I get the phone call. I meet with them. I take two people that I think are sharp and that would understand the local foods. We meet with Farm Aid. They give us the parameters. We put the proposal together, and we won. It was the first time they ever used a contract dining company versus local restaurants.

Since 2016, Parkhurst Dining has been the food service provider for Farm Aid concerts.

"I rented an RV, and Justin Betzer, our chef, stayed in the parking lot for seven nights straight. Didn't come out. Didn't blink an eye. We blew them away, totally, with how organized we were. The culture, the food, the local farmers, our detail to people.

"We weren't out of there until 2:00 or 3:00 in the morning. When Farm Aid was done, we met at the Robinson Eat'n Park at 7:00 on Sunday morning. That was the best time for all of us, no matter how tired we were. 'What'd we do well? What did we not do well?'

"So, the next year Farm Aid took us to Connecticut. We didn't have a choice. They said, 'You're doing Connecticut.' We had all our notes from the previous year. We were ready to go. And in 2019, we did Wisconsin.

"A few months in advance, we went up to the venue. Then we went around with Farm Aid to meet with all the local farmers. Most of the meetings were cold calls on local farms. We drove around, and our chefs and Farm Aid had conversations with the farmers. 'What products do you have? Can we offer it at Farm Aid because we feature local products?' And most of the products are donated for Farm Aid. Our chefs are so good, they don't know what that menu's going to be until a week or two before. And then, they put it all together. The team is phenomenal.

"During Farm Aid, we provide food service for the artists and the support team. It's such a down-to-earth group of people: Neil Young, John Mellencamp, and so on. There are no special riders. And it's for a good cause – to enrich the farmers' lives, to make them successful, farm to market.

"We start on the Tuesday before the concert because they start setting up the stage. We start with 200 for breakfast, lunch, and dinner. By Thursday we're up to 500 for breakfast, lunch, and dinner. Friday, it's 1,000 for breakfast, lunch, and dinner. Saturday it's 2,000 because all the artists and the groups come in. It's 1,000 of the artists and staff, plus 1,000 VIPs. There are no kitchens. So, we design a kitchen and bring it in. Design everything from scratch. And we execute it perfectly."

Parkhurst has continued to hit the right note with Farm Aid, as its services were engaged again for the 2022 event.

"It's fun. It's different. It's unique. And the team loves doing it. When I have a team like that, I know we're going to succeed."

~~~~~~

"It's 1,000 of the artists and staff, plus 1,000 VIPs. There are no kitchens. So, we design a kitchen and bring it in. Design everything from scratch. And we execute it perfectly."

— Bryan Marince

~~~~~~

The Past as Prologue

Staying committed to the founding principles, by 2022 Parkhurst had 80 client partners across 15 states, from New England to Virginia to Illinois. Its diverse clients range from small, private colleges to banks and insurance providers.

"Our biggest differentiator in our industry is that we invest in relationships," says Suzie Lachut, managing director of growth and retention at Parkhurst. "People know Jeff and Mark by name. They will see them on campus. They'll see Larry Orr, our vice president of higher education. They'll see Ken McIntyre, our vice president of corporate dining," she explains. "We're real people, and we're authentic. That reputation precedes us, and our reputation for retention of

Suzie Lachut attributes Parkhurst's success, in part, to investing in relationships.

clients and investing in those relationships strengthens our ability to continue to grow."

"We have people that care about what we're doing and about quality contracts and about not changing our game plan," Nick Camody adds. "At the end of the day, we still believe in our food, our service, and creating that smile."

Added Dimensions

While Parkhurst was growing, Eat'n Park Hospitality Group was growing hungry for a new concept. It was 2003, and an opportunity was taking shape in Pittsburgh's Cultural District.

"It was an opportunity for us to put our thumbprint downtown," Jeff remembers, "and on a corner that was a void for the city. We saw it as an opportunity to enhance the overall downtown image."

There was another motivation. "It gave my brother Mark an opportunity to come back to Pittsburgh," Jeff says. The downtown space was a blank canvas. "It was perfect for Mark's creativity – something new, something more upscale." That, combined with Parkhurst's growth, made it the right time to reunite the Broadhurst brothers.

Like Jeff and Brooks, Mark was formally trained in hospitality administration. After graduating from Cornell University, he decided to learn more about the culinary aspect of hospitality and enrolled at Le Cordon Bleu in Paris. To complete his knowledge of the hospitality industry (at least, that's what he told his parents), he enrolled in beer brewing school at Chicago's Siebel Institute of Technology.

With his credentials earned, Mark began his professional career working as the director of operations at Kahunaville Management, a restaurant and entertainment chain based in Delaware. He joined Kahunaville when there was one location, and he was instrumental in expanding the chain to include locations throughout the country. Mark's frequent flyer miles kept pace with the company's expansion, geographically spanning from Philadelphia to Las Vegas.

Mark's experience with Kahunaville, combined with his knowledge of Eat'n Park and its values, made him the perfect choice for developing the Pittsburgh based company's new concepts. With a little convincing from his family, Mark gave up his jet-setting career with Kahunaville for an equally exciting opportunity – devoting his energy and creativity to the development of the company's first new-concept restaurant and, later, to the growth of Parkhurst Dining.

As director of concept development, Mark led the team that created Six Penn Kitchen, the company's first foray into downtown Pittsburgh. He and Jim Broadhurst crossed the country researching restaurant designs, operations, ambience, and menus. "We wanted to demonstrate that, as a company, we could create a dining experience different from Eat'n Park restaurants," Mark explains. "In some ways, the food we were creating at Parkhurst inspired the menu at Six Penn."

Elements of the Six Penn Kitchen concept took shape at a restaurant near the company's headquarters. "Mark would sit at the bar drawing sketches on cocktail napkins," remembers Meg Straub, who, at that time, was a manager at the restaurant. "He was so excited, and we thought he was nuts!"

In 2005, Mark and his team introduced Six Penn Kitchen. Although the restaurant had great success, its earliest days could have closed the restaurant before it opened.

"We were slated to host the Pittsburgh Symphony gala," remembers Meg, who got over her doubts about Mark's cocktail drawings and joined the Six Penn team. "We expected to be open in time for the gala, but there were a series of setbacks that delayed our opening."

The gala is one of Pittsburgh's more prestigious social events. With only weeks until the event, there was no turning back for the restaurant. Even though the restaurant wasn't open, the Six Penn team opened the doors for the gala guests.

"We had a slate concrete floor," Meg explains. "We had plastic covering unfinished sections. And we rented everything – tables, chairs, linens, everything. Women were in ball gowns in a construction site! Many things could have gone wrong, but it ended up being a successful launch of the restaurant. It was a bunch of scrappy people that made it work."

Meg believes that "scrappy" attitude resulted from the building that housed Six Penn. It was an old building that originally had five floors. Years earlier, people were killed in a fire that destroyed the top two levels of the building. According to Meg, "There's an urban legend that the building is haunted."

The spirits served on Six Penn's rooftop made it a popular gathering spot during warm months. However, team members had to climb three flights of stairs carrying food and beverages to reach the rooftop, which helped to strengthen leg muscles and that scrappy attitude.

"It really was a team," Meg says. "Everyone considered it their house, they were family. And they did it for Mark. His vision was inspiring, and they wanted to make it happen for him."

Six Penn Kitchen was open for 13 years. It was perfect for business lunches, pre-show dining, and post-game celebrating, and it was a key element in the revival of the city's downtown dining scene.

Six Penn Kitchen closed in 2018. That "scrappy" team remains a team years after the restaurant's closing. "A lot of the core people who were with the restaurant since the earliest days are like family," Meg says. "They get together on weekends, they vacation together, they go through life together."

"We had a great run," Mark explains, "but it was time to focus on the growth of other concepts." That included Parkhurst Dining.

On the final night of operation, Six Penn Kitchen team members celebrated the restaurant's 13-year run.

New in the Neighborhood

Mark also led the creation of a second, new-brand concept – The Porch at Schenley – that opened in November 2011. The path toward the opening had many curves.

"We were looking for something that would be a new concept. We looked at our marketplace and what different segments of guests were looking for," Mark remembers. "We did a lot of research and brought in a lot of consultants, including a Hollywood movie set designer and a Seattle brand specialist. We spent two days locked away and came up with different ideas and settled on some ideas for the new prototype.

The team knew they wanted the new restaurant to emphasize convenience and speed. "The menu would be designed around food that takes a lot of time to prep and develop, but when you order, it's served quickly," Mark explains.

They also wanted guests to be able to see into the kitchen so they could watch food being prepared. A pickup window would add to convenience, and an ideal setting would provide an option for outdoor seating.

While the new concept was still being refined, Mark was approached by the Pittsburgh Parks Conservancy about the possibility of opening a restaurant on property it owned in the Oakland section of Pittsburgh. Mark was intrigued. He and his team had a prototype in development, and although they hadn't moved forward with it, he knew it would be perfect for this location. "We wanted a high-density place that was meant for people who wanted speed," Mark says. "I knew that Oakland would be the perfect place for that, where you have all these people during the day who need speed to get in and out, but at night, you're drawing people who might want to sit back and relax."

Before ground could be broken, Eat'n Park Hospitality Group had to go through a long approval process. "We needed to get the city to approve a building on a public piece of land that's run by a nonprofit and is in a historic district," Mark explains. "And we spent a lot of time working out the details with the Parks Conservancy. I think we had 28 versions of the lease and terms."

One of the directives from the Parks Conservancy was to design a restaurant that blended into the neighboring park. The challenge was met, from both an exterior and interior perspective.

Once the approvals and agreements were in place, the final concept was created. The restaurant would adapt its pace to match the changing speeds of Oakland visitors and residents, with a walk-up window for breakfast, a quick-service style for lunch, and a relaxing sit-down style for dinner. The restaurant would showcase local foods and sustainable practices, including a rooftop apiary whose bees would provide honey for food and beverages, and a rooftop garden whose produce would be used in the restaurant's salads, beverages, and entrees. And the restaurant design would enable guests to enjoy the park setting, whether they were around the fireplace or out in the sunshine.

On a cold November day in 2011, The Porch at Schenley opened.

"So a place that was meant to be capitalizing on the outside experience was not all that busy for the first five months," Mark remembers. "And in my mind, I was saying, 'When it gets nice, when it gets nice. This is gonna be busy, it's gonna be a great spot.' I was keeping my fingers crossed."

During the first week of March 2012 the temperature in Oakland reached 70 degrees. "The floodgates opened, and it's been busy ever since," Mark says with a smile.

Building on the success of The Porch at Schenley, The Porch at Siena opened in the South Hills suburbs of Pittsburgh in the summer of 2017.

Saying Hello to Old Favorites and New Friends

In between the openings of The Porch at Schenley and The Porch at Siena, another concept was born: Concept X. Planning the new concept actually began before the opportunity for The Porch at Schenley arose.

"We wanted to introduce a new growth concept," Mark Broadhurst explains, "and we saw opportunities in areas around the city that were growing."

Mark and his colleagues knew they wanted to leverage what people love most about Eat'n Park and package it differently. As they researched what those menu items were and the audience they hoped to attract, they began to see how Concept X might take shape: it would be a fast-casual restaurant with personality.

"Initially, we were thinking we'd take the Eat'n Park classics and introduce other items," Mark says. "But our concept kept getting bigger. We had to scale back because we wanted something simpler than Eat'n Park."

The result was Hello Bistro, a casual restaurant with a sassy attitude. The menu is an adaptation of the two most popular items on the Eat'n Park menu – the Soup, Salad & Fruit Bar and burgers. Each provides a focus on customization. "We want everything on our Hello Bistro menu to have a build-your-own flair to it," explains Mercy Senchur, chief operating officer, Restaurant Division.

The design of Hello Bistro restaurants reinforces the restaurants' personality while providing a functional space for guests and team members.

"Restaurants are so complex," Andy Dunmire explains. As the architect who heads Eat'n Park's Design & Construction Department, Andy has first-hand experience with complexities. It's knowledge that took root at an early age. "My grandfather owned a lumberyard, so I was always there. I knew how building parts and pieces went together," he recalls. "I knew I was going to be an architect before I knew there was a name for it."

With thoughtful guidance from art teachers, Andy's interest and skill increased. After earning a degree in architecture, he perfected his craft with challenging projects at architectural firms. When he joined Eat'n Park, he quickly discovered a new set of challenges. "With restaurants, you're dealing with people's behaviors and habits. There's an appreciation for who the people are."

Andy and his team need to anticipate what those behaviors and habits might be when they are designing a new restaurant concept. "When you have a new restaurant concept, a lot of people start with a clean slate," Andy explains. But when Andy and his colleagues began exploring a new restaurant concept in 2007, they started with something better than a clean slate.

Andy began the design of Hello Bistro by considering how much space would be needed, what equipment would be necessary, what the service model would be, and how the line would queue. The answers would help him determine the arrangement of the restaurant. Andy turned to a standard tool for architects – bubble diagrams – which helped him to plot space, guest circulation, and how one element related to the next.

The process was a collaborative effort, with the realization that each decision would affect the design. "The amount that the built environment can influence a guest is incredible," Andy says. "It's very powerful that you have the ability to design elements and set the stage for expectations without people even recognizing it."

Andy Dunmire led a team that combined science and art in developing the design of Hello Bistro.

When the details of the new salad and burger concept were coming into focus, the team decided to test the initial design by creating a mock-up in the Corporate Support Center. They created a type of salad bar by placing various crocks of food in the order they believed would guide the guests' journey. "We didn't want to have names on all the ingredients because we thought that detracted from the food," Andy explains. "We really wanted the food to be upfront and central to the concept. The hero of the visuals was the salad bar with all the fresh ingredients right up front for the guests to see."

With the mock-up fully set, people from the corporate office were invited to enjoy lunch. "We really learned a lot by videotaping how the flow went, how the conversations went, the interaction between the guests," Andy says.

An early sketch of the design of Hello Bistro

Hello Bistro was introduced in the Oakland section of Pittsburgh in 2012. The restaurant's edgy personality was created through design, branding, and hiring the right people. "Mercy Senchur knows how to hire for the right attitude, the right energy," Andy says. Décor, messaging, uniforms, and name tags all reinforce the edginess.

Andy sums it up: "It's not just what the built environment is. It's understanding who your guest is and who your team member is, and making the environment very comfortable, seamless, and enjoyable to be in."

6

Giving Birth to a Parent Company

Eat'n Park Hospitality Group

By 2000, Eat'n Park had outgrown its once spacious offices in Robinson Township. The company moved to a recently opened development, The Waterfront in Homestead, located south of Pittsburgh in an area once defined by steel. With long-deserted smokestacks as its centerpiece, the new development was banking on an influx of businesses, retail shops, hotels, and restaurants to establish a new economy for the struggling boroughs of Homestead, Munhall, and West Homestead.

Suzy and Jim Broadhurst

"The Waterfront was one site where we could get a huge piece of property that would accommodate both our offices and our Eat'n Park restaurant," Jim Broadhurst explains. "When we were in Robinson Township, we learned the benefits of having our headquarters and training center together. Although an office did not require prime space, the restaurant certainly did."

There was another benefit to locating in the new development. "In the back of our minds, we knew this had the potential to be a really successful development for the whole community," Jim adds.

Eat'n Park Hospitality Group Corporate Support Center is located at The Waterfront in Homestead, Pennsylvania.

The announcement of the new location for the company was not met with immediate enthusiasm. "Half the office was saying, 'Homestead? Why are we going to Homestead? Why so far away?'" Keith Lester, retired district manager, remembers. "But Jim Broadhurst was able to see then that we could become what we are today."

On November 16, 2000, Eat'n Park's new Corporate Support Center (CSC) opened at The Waterfront, with an Eat'n Park restaurant on the adjacent property. It was more than a new address; it was a new era for the corporation. The Corporate Support Center houses all the functions that help each of the divisions to operate. The CSC staff are not only supporting guests, they also are supporting team members. "We not only changed the name of our headquarters," Jim explains, "we revitalized our philosophy about customer support."

A number of different business divisions were operating out of the Corporate Support Center. In addition to Eat'n Park Restaurants, Park Classic Diners, Parkhurst Dining, Cura Hospitality, SmileyCookie.com, and Brysco were part of the family. To call the company Eat'n Park Restaurants no longer reflected the diversity of operations.

In 2001, the company's leadership established a new structure to accommodate the diversification. Eat'n Park Hospitality Group was christened with two divisions – the Restaurant Division and the On-Site Brands Division. Not only did the name of the parent company better reflect the breadth of the entity, it also was broad enough that, if any other business units were created, they could easily fall under the Hospitality Group umbrella.

The Restaurant Division at the time included Eat'n Park, as well as Park Classic Diners. Jeff Broadhurst assumed the presidency of the Restaurant Division when Basil Cox was promoted to vice chairman of Eat'n Park Hospitality Group in 2006. Previously, Jeff had served as president of Parkhurst Dining.

The On-Site Brands Division comprised Parkhurst Dining and Cura. Mitch Possinger, the founder and president of Cura, was appointed president of On-Site Brands in 2006.

The leadership committed their passion to paper: Eat'n Park Hospitality Group's vision is "to be the best multi-concept food service company in our region." The mission of the corporation is "to profitably build and strengthen our brands by delivering exceptional dining experiences through a diverse, well-trained, and motivated team."

The Next Generation

By 2008, all three Broadhurst sons had been working together in the family business for five years. Jeff was president of the Restaurant Division; Brooks was managing the supply chain for the Restaurant Division and Parkhurst Dining; and Mark was spearheading new concept development.

Eat'n Park restaurants were flourishing in Pennsylvania, Ohio, and West Virginia; Parkhurst and Cura were established and growing; and Six Penn Kitchen, the company's first foray into upscale dining, was a popular spot in Pittsburgh's Cultural District.

The time was right for a change.

Under Jim Broadhurst's direction, Eat'n Park Restaurants evolved to reflect the changing needs of the marketplace. He led the evolution from carhop dining to family restaurants to a multi-faceted hospitality group; he oversaw menu development, including the introduction of salad bars, Smiley Cookies, and in-restaurant bakeries; and the company had developed multiple business units. He and his wife, Suzy, created a spirit of

Eat'n Park Hospitality Group appointed Jeff Broadhurst to succeed his father as president and CEO.

philanthropy throughout the organization, pledging 5% of pre-tax profits to community support and spearheading campaigns that have generated tens of millions of dollars for children's hospitals and United Way.

In March 2008, Jim announced his retirement as president and CEO of Eat'n Park Hospitality Group, while retaining his position as chairman. In turn, the privately held company's Board of Directors approved the appointment of Jeff Broadhurst to the position being vacated by his father.

The Leadership Path

Like all the Broadhurst brothers, Jeff's career with Eat'n Park began in an Eat'n Park restaurant. When he was in high school, Jeff worked at the South Park restaurant as a cook. His specialty? "I could make good grilled cheese sandwiches – the easiest thing on the menu," he laughs.

What started out as a job to earn spending money became a calling. "A year or two into it, I realized I really enjoyed it," Jeff explains. "That's when I went into the hotel and hospitality management school at Cornell." He quickly followed that degree with an MBA from the Katz Graduate School of Business at the University of Pittsburgh.

That phone call Jeff received from his father inviting him to join the company was followed by an interview with Dan Wilson. Jeff knew the opportunity to lead the sales effort for Parkhurst was the right opportunity at the right time.

As Parkhurst expanded, Jeff assumed the presidency of the fledgling company – an advancement, he contends, that didn't change much. "I don't know that I thought much differently about it," he says. "It was the first time I really led something, but it really was about the team."

Jeff's second experience in a leadership role was when he was appointed president of Eat'n Park Restaurants. Admittedly, he felt some pressure. He was following in his father's footsteps – a man beloved, respected, and known by just about everyone in the company. "That move was a little more challenging at the beginning," Jeff says. "I knew people were watching closely."

Jeff's rise to the top position was well planned. He gained experience in several key departments on the restaurant side of the business, including information technology, strategic planning, and finance. "I bounced around the company," Jeff says. "It may have been that I enjoyed new things, so I'd raise my hand and say, 'Yeah, I'd like to do that, I'd like to oversee that, I'd like to get involved in that.'" That willingness – combined with his experience, acumen, and exposure – positioned Jeff to assume the role of president and CEO of Eat'n Park Hospitality Group.

Jeff's second experience in a leadership role was when he was appointed president of Eat'n Park Restaurants. He was following in his father's footsteps – a man beloved, respected, and known by just about everyone in the company.

A Defined Succession Plan

The CEO leadership transition was the final stage in a well-defined succession plan. Basil Cox had retired as president and chief operating officer of the restaurant division. Dave Wohleber retired as chief financial officer and was succeeded by Dan Wilson. Chuck Sites had shared overseeing restaurant operations with Dale Springer. When Chuck retired as vice president of operations, Mercy Senchur joined Dale in co-directing operations.

The retirements of (left to right) Basil Cox, Dave Wohleber, and Chuck Sites led to a new executive leadership team.

Each move occurred only when successors were firmly in place. "We planned these changes in a way that allowed for continuity," Jim explains. "There was no break in momentum, no change in culture."

Keith Lester, who experienced the leadership of Larry Hatch, Bill Peters, Bob Moore, Jim Broadhurst, and Basil Cox, understood why the board chose Jeff to lead the company. "When Jeff was first promoted to president of Parkhurst, I made the comment to a close work associate that I was really disappointed that he was taking over Parkhurst. I wanted him to take over all of Eat'n Park because he is the perfect blend of his father's intellect and vision and his mother's compassion and customer service."

Reflecting on his parents' influence, Jeff says, "My dad has taught me how to respect people. He's taught me to always look at the positive, but to never stop trying to do better; to celebrate every success, but to honestly critique myself. I've learned a lot from my dad."

He continues, "My mother always told us to treat people how we like to be treated. She told us not to get too full of ourselves. And she told us to always take time to enjoy dessert – especially cookies and milk."

"When Jeff was first promoted to president of Parkhurst, I made the comment to a close work associate that I was really disappointed that he was taking over Parkhurst. I wanted him to take over all of Eat'n Park because he is the perfect blend of his father's intellect and vision and his mother's compassion and customer service."

— Keith Lester

7

An Appetite for Pleasing Palates

At its core, a restaurant is about food. For Eat'n Park – and, more recently, Hello Bistro, Parkhurst Dining, and The Porch – food is a blend of understanding guests' interests, anticipating trends, incorporating innovations, and pleasing palates.

Early Classics

On opening day in 1949, Eat'n Park's menu included the soon-to-be-popular Big Boy and specialties like cube steak sandwiches and 'Ham Bar-B-Que.' Cincinnati-based Frisch's had inspired Larry Hatch to introduce the Big Boy, and it wasn't long before Eat'n Park adapted another item from Frisch's menu – the Brawny Lad.

With Germanic roots, the Brawny Lad quickly became a favorite with Eat'n Park guests. The popular sandwich began with a tender steak grilled to order and served on a toasted sesame-seed bun with a generous slice of sweet onion. By the mid-1970s, the sandwich had run its course and was removed from the menu. Legend has it that occasionally, long-time guests will ask their server if they can order a Brawny Lad.

Trade Mark

Frisch's Brawny Lad was the inspiration for a popular menu item at Eat'n Park.

The first menus ensured that anyone's sweet tooth could be satisfied with a dessert selection that included "cruellers," banana splits, and doughnuts. "In those days, doughnuts were the big item at breakfast," Bob Moore remembered. "When the doughnut company started to raise their prices, I got the bright idea of making our own. We tried this with a timed fryer in the basement," he continued. "We made some fancy doughnuts, and they were very good, but what a mess and what a pain in the neck to produce. We quickly decided that the doughnut company was undercharging us!"

Appealing Spuds

Throughout the first several decades, Eat'n Park guests had a choice of potatoes: French fries or French fries. "That was the only potato we had – breakfast, lunch, and dinner," Bob Moore explained. Preparation of the fries began with fresh, whole potatoes that were peeled by an unusual machine. "It looked like an old clothes washer," Bob said. "It was a tub with rough cement sides on the inside. With the potatoes in, you turned on the machine and it would rotate very fast. This would throw the potatoes against the rough sides, which would remove the potato skins." However, if the potatoes were left in the machine too long, they were reduced to the size of a marble.

The peeled potatoes were cut by hand into French fries, then blanched, placed in a frying basket, and partially cooked. The process was time consuming, taking most of the team members' morning hours. Once completed, the team arranged the French fries on trays and placed them in the cooler. The frozen potatoes then were fried for the finished product. "For some reason we didn't use timers, and we sure didn't have computers. We felt we could tell by looking. If done right," Bob noted, "the fresh French fries were delicious, but very inconsistent in quality."

Throughout the first several decades, Eat'n Park guests had a choice of potatoes: French fries or French fries. "That was the only potato we had – breakfast, lunch, and dinner," Bob Moore explained.

A Crisp Addition

In the late 1960s/early 1970s, restaurant owners began looking at lettuce as more than a leafy vegetable; they started to see it as a way to present guests with two sought-after elements: healthy food choices and the ability to customize. It was the birth of the salad bar.

Eat'n Park introduced a salad bar in 1975 at the New Castle restaurant. The bar was on wheels and kept in the back of the restaurant until lunchtime, when servers wheeled the small bar into the dining area.

Seeing an opportunity, Eat'n Park began expanding salad bars to its other locations in 1978. New Castle's trial led the way to today's Soup, Salad & Fruit Bar.

Over the years, Eat'n Park has expanded the salad bar offerings. Today, guests can customize their salad experience with warm soups, freshly baked bread, and produce and fruit that is locally sourced, when available. On weekend mornings, the bar is expanded to include the Breakfast Buffet.

Today, the Soup, Salad & Fruit Bar is the most popular item on Eat'n Park's menu, with the Superburger running a close second.

On the Go for a Good Cup of Joe

At the height of Eat'n Park's coffee-house days, the beverage sold for a dime a cup and did not include refills. And that created a problem. Bob Moore explained, "If the customer emptied their cup and wanted another coffee, 10¢ was added to the check. It was when the customer asked for a warm-up that it became a problem. What is a warm-up? One-half cup? Three-quarters of a cup, or what? This problem was never solved, so we ignored it."

More recently, coffee posed a different problem for Brooks Broadhurst. Brooks likes coffee, but he didn't think Eat'n Park's coffee was as good as it should be.

"I thought it was not very tasty at all," Brooks says. "It was bad."

So Brooks, who was then the vice president of purchasing, set out to change that in 2010. He began by writing to his father who, at the time, was chairman and CEO, and to Basil Cox, who was president. "It's a critically important product," he lobbied, "so we have got to have better coffee!"

The elder Broadhurst and Basil agreed with Brooks, and so began a process to improve the restaurant's coffee. Bill Swoope, the owner of The Coffee Tree Roasters, had a relationship with Hacienda La Minita, a plantation in Los Santos, Costa Rica. He invited Brooks to visit the supplier's plantation. Brooks was already buying espresso from The Coffee Tree Roasters for some of the hospitality group's Parkhurst Dining clients.

Brooks, Basil Cox, and Nick Camody, the chief operating officer of Parkhurst, dusted off their passports and headed south.

Once in Costa Rica and after his first sip, Basil understood why he had just traveled more than 2,000 miles for a cup of coffee. "You're right," he said to Brooks. "This coffee is spectacular."

The plantation's approach added to the quality of the coffee flavor. "They are one of the very few vertically integrated coffee producers," Brooks explains. "They grow their own coffee, they roast it, grind it, and sell it. Most people either grow it and sell it or they buy it and roast it."

The coffee caravan returned to Pittsburgh with work to do. They began by testing the new coffee in a handful of restaurants that had high coffee sales. "Some restaurants, no one said anything," Brooks says. "Some we had complaints, some we had positives." But there was one location where guests were livid.

Brooks Broadhurst led the effort to improve the taste of Eat'n Park's coffee.

Brooks decided to visit the restaurant so he could hear the complaints firsthand. He brought three packets of the new coffee and three packets of the original coffee with him and gave them to the restaurant manager.

He asked the manager to brew them both. "Brew them in exactly the same way, then bring them out. And I don't want to know which is which."

There were a dozen or so guests seated at the restaurant's counter, agitated by the sight of the guy who changed their coffee. The manager served each of them a cup of the original coffee and a cup of the new coffee.

"Everyone is trying it, and they're saying, 'Oh I know which one it is.' 'No, I'm sure.' 'Yep, this is the one,'" Brooks recalls.

One by one they all pointed out their preferred coffee which – although they didn't know it – was the new coffee. All but one of the guests in the blind taste test preferred the new brew.

"My goal was to have people drinking a really good cup of coffee," Brooks concludes. "Either you have coffee for breakfast, so it's the first thing you have when you get to the restaurant, or you have it after dinner, and it's the last thing you have. And so," he says, "you want your first impression or your last impression to be good."

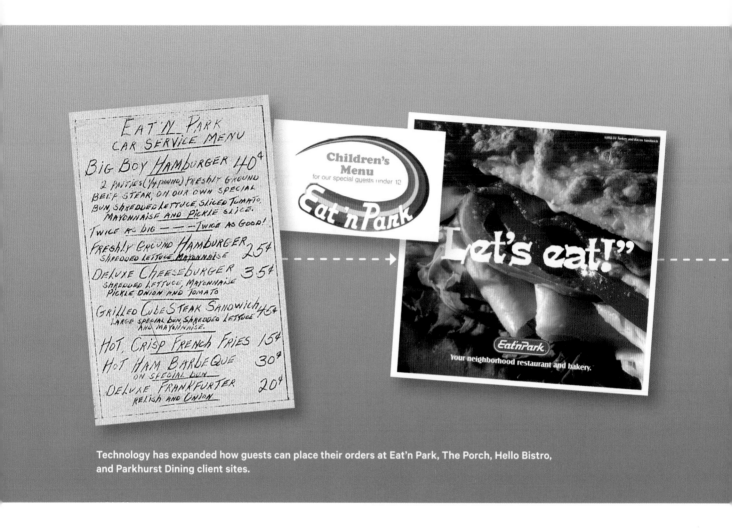

Technology has expanded how guests can place their orders at Eat'n Park, The Porch, Hello Bistro, and Parkhurst Dining client sites.

A Recipe for Success

Eat'n Park's opening day menu was a handwritten list that included eight sandwiches, seven entrees ("plates"), and five sides. The format of today's menus have not only evolved to full-color printed and digital options, the variety of offerings has also expanded.

What guests see on menus is only part of today's Eat'n Park Hospitality Group food story. Behind the photos of mouth-watering selections is a complex process that involves multiple disciplines and exhaustive research.

"At the core of what we do is strive to create a smile and provide an enjoyable experience for our guests," explains Amanda Giacobbi, senior director of marketing, Restaurant Division. "When you're a consistent brand that's been around for seven decades, menu development is important."

Deciding what was on the menu was a rather informal process until the mid-1980s, when John Vichie was named director of product development. His years working in the restaurants gave him a special talent. "The one thing that John knew for sure was the tastes of our guests," remembers Carol Kijanka, formerly John's executive assistant. "He knew what guests would like, and he would look far ahead to what he thought guests would like in six months, a year. I don't know how he did it."

In his new role, John tapped into that talent and put in place a thoughtful menu development process. He wanted to elevate the quality of Eat'n Park food and began by introducing a food manual to help to ensure consistency among the restaurants.

"It was an interesting time," Carol says. "Eat'n Park was on the cusp of changing." In his new position, John accelerated that change. "He decided that he wasn't fond of a lot of our food," Carol continues. "So, he started by changing the French fries and ground beef. As time progressed, he created many recipes. In fact, several of the soups we have today – including our chicken noodle soup – are pretty much the same soups he created."

Pittsburgh personality and one-time Eat'n Park team member Larry Richert is framed by former and current directors of menu development, Chef Regis Holden and Chef John Frick.

Following John's untimely death, Basil Cox promoted Regis Holden from director, procurement and safety, to director, menu development for Eat'n Park Restaurants. Building on John Vichie's foundation, Regis successfully expanded the menu development process by adding new systems and procedures to score and rate guest comments through a matrix approach. His work led to similar processes for the distinct needs of Hello Bistro and The Porch.

Regis also created menu development committees for each brand, which continue today. Each restaurant brand's committee typically includes restaurant operators to gauge the complexity of items that are under development; a marketing representative to consider how the item will be received by targeted audiences; and a supply chain representative who can evaluate the availability of an ingredient and where they are going to source it. There's always a chef, a trainer, and the chief operating officer, who unites all the disciplines and calculates the financial implications of menu considerations.

After Regis's retirement in 2019, John Frick was promoted to director, menu development. John explains that the work of the menu development committee centers around one question: what is it that we are trying to achieve?

The answers are shaped not only by industry trends, but also by flavor trends, ingredient development, pricing trends, guest interest, and team member feedback. "Every other month we have a meeting where we're presenting recipes, ideas, and procedure changes. We want to make sure that our team members can execute a new item consistently and that we have menu items that appeal to a broad range of folks," John explains.

"We build around the core menu with seasonal items," Mercy Senchur says. "That's what we try to do with all of our restaurant brands – Eat'n Park, Hello Bistro, and The Porch. We remain fresh by making sure that we're very seasonal, but the core menu items stay strong and continue to be the focus."

"And we want to be sure that the new item feels like something that's intuitive and related to our brand," Amanda adds.

Once the recipes are perfected, the members of the menu development committee meet in the test kitchen, located near the company's Corporate Support Center. "The beauty of the test kitchen is that everyone is right there," John explains. "We can interact while I'm preparing the item. And the operations people can begin thinking about what it would look like in their restaurants' kitchens."

The next step in the menu development process at Eat'n Park is testing the item in select restaurants. Guests' ratings and product sales help to determine if an item makes its way onto the menu.

When the menu development committee gives the green light to a new menu item, the final step is team member training. Every time there's a menu change, team members need to be trained, from greeters, to servers, to the kitchen. They need to know how to make the new item, how to sell it, and how to explain it to a guest.

John Vichie developed many menu items that are still popular today.

"We work with our training team to put together the training materials," John says. "Videos, photographs, whatever is necessary, to support team members so they can roll it out effectively."

"Every other month we have a meeting where we're presenting recipes, ideas, and procedure changes. We want to make sure that our team members can execute a new item consistently and that we have menu items that appeal to a broad range of folks."

— John Frick

Moving an Entrée Upstream

To move a new menu item from the test kitchen to dozens of restaurants and, ultimately, to guests, requires precise execution. Consider one of Eat'n Park's more popular menu items – the Whale of a Cod. Each restaurant must replicate the sandwich that John Frick creates in his test kitchen. The individual restaurants receive all the raw materials, including the hand-cut cod filet. At each restaurant, the cooks coat the filet in a special panko bread crumb batter, then place the cod in a 350-degree deep fryer. Two minutes later, the filet is dressed to become a Whale of a Cod.

There are no short cuts, John explains. "We really have some tremendous prep people with all the brands who just do a phenomenal job. They care so much about what they do and work to make it the best they can every day. Those are the inspiring things that make me want to continue to develop menu items that they can be successful with so that they continue to grow."

Developing new menu items is essential, but some menu items, like Whale of a Cod, Superburgers, and potato soup, have become legendary for Eat'n Park guests.

Amanda Giacobbi explains, "When you ask someone about Eat'n Park, sometimes they'll say, 'Oh, I love the ranch dressing,' or 'Oh, I love the Superburger.' But more often than not, they're going to share a historical story about how they went to Eat'n Park every Friday when they were in high school, or they went there every Sunday after church with their grandparents, or they now take their child there after their dentist appointments. There's an emotional component to us being a part of the community and a part of people's lives. To have that passion and brand advocacy is so unique."

Developing new menu items is essential, but some menu items, like Whale of a Cod, Superburgers, and potato soup, have become legendary for Eat'n Park guests.

Understanding Guests' Preferences

Despite exhaustive research and testing, occasionally, something makes it onto a menu that doesn't generate the expected demand. Espresso at Eat'n Park and wine and beer at Hello Bistro are examples.

"If it's not working, it's important to exit. It's as important to exit an item as it is to add an item," Mercy Senchur explains. However, she vividly remembers a time when they removed an item a little too quickly.

"Chili in the summer," she says laughing. "We took chili off the menu for the summer and replaced it with another soup. Oh, my Lord, did the phones ring off the hook! It was unbelievable. We heard our guests, and we brought it back."

"It's as important to exit an item as it is to add an item," Mercy explains.

Although details may change from brand to brand, one thing remains unchanged. "That same joy sentiment and that same inspiration of creating a smile is consistent throughout the brands," Amanda notes. "So, whether a guest is enjoying an Eat'n Park classic like a Superburger, experiencing a salad at Hello Bistro for the first time, or sitting outside at The Porch listening to live music, our goal is to create a hospitable experience that makes guests happy."

Picking up New Options

In its earliest years, Eat'n Park restaurant carhops would deliver food to guests in their cars. About 40 years after Eat'n Park ended carhop service, the restaurant returned to serving guests in their cars – this time through pickup windows.

Although pickup windows were common at fast-food restaurants, Eat'n Park was the first dine-in restaurant in the region to introduce them. The first opened at the Monroeville Eat'n Park in 2008.

Pickup windows made the dining experience more convenient for guests and didn't compromise the quality of the food. The company leaders considered other options first, including a drive-thru option and curbside service. They rejected drive thru because it would have required food to be prepared in advance, and the menu would be limited – two factors that didn't support the Eat'n Park brand. Curbside service simply wasn't convenient enough.

The opening of the Monroeville pickup window shattered sales records. Soon, Eat'n Park began introducing windows at every location where it was feasible. By 2022, there were pickup windows at 48 restaurants, and new construction and renovations include the addition of pickup windows, wherever possible.

"We knew that pickup windows were going to be a growth area for us," Jeff Broadhurst explains. "But we never could have anticipated just how important they would be to our business."

A Different Brand with Different Goals

"The two sides of our business are the same, yet they're very different," explains Dave Beauvais, vice president, supply chain, speaking about the Restaurant Division and Parkhurst Dining. That means that the menu development process is slightly different for each of the Hospitality Group's brands. In the Restaurant Division, consistency among locations is essential. Within Parkhurst, each client location provides a unique experience.

"We use Parkhurst's culinary gold standards to understand what we can and should source for Parkhurst," explains Dave "When the standard requires that Parkhurst client sites serve fresh French fries or that soup stock is made from scratch, those are standards that give us clarity on what we should be buying."

Parkhurst primarily serves colleges, universities, and corporations. Each chef at a Parkhurst site determines the menu based on client feedback and budget.

"Since Parkhurst started, we've always had some type of a culinary development team," explains Chris Fitz, district manager with Parkhurst Dining. "We bring chefs together to collaborate. Historically, it's been primarily some of the tenured folks that really embrace change and have helped drive us. What we're seeing now is more participation from some of the newer folks who are giving us ideas."

"We use Parkhurst's culinary gold standards to understand what we can and should source for Parkhurst."

— Dave Beauvais, vice president, supply chain

"If a student asks me to put something on the menu tonight, I'm going to try to make it happen," says Lee Keener, general manager for Parkhurst Dining at Valparaiso University. "We live for that kind of challenge."

For Bill Jones, the director of catering for Parkhurst at PNC Tower, the clientele is vastly different from that found on college campuses. Much of his work is based on business meetings. In a typical year, Parkhurst can cater more than 1,200 events at just one of PNC's corporate locations. They range from a coffee break for two people to a three-day conference for two hundred people. Whatever the occasion, the quality of the food is paramount.

"PNC leaves it up to the person organizing the event to choose what they want to make their group happy," Bill explains. "If it needs to be vegetarian, more organic, more plant-based, fantastic, do it. If another group wants tater tots and cheese sauce, fantastic, do it. Just make them happy."

"It's all about passion," Chris adds. "We're passionate about making great food and delivering great experiences."

Parkhurst Dining chefs Lee Keener, Marcy Fickes, and Dan Chiaverini

How clients define "great food" has changed over time. Today's college dining experience is all about options. On college campuses, bland cafeterias with homogenous menu staples like macaroni and cheese, roast beef and gravy, and liver and onions have given way to lively food courts with a variety of Parkhurst-branded stations with options that could include vegan, plant based, pescatarian, and allergen free.

The evolution is attributed to a more sophisticated palate and a more educated consumer. "The students we feed today are a lot more educated about food," says Marcy Fickes, executive chef for Parkhurst Dining at Mercyhurst University. "They care about what's in food. They care about the people that serve them. They're more involved, they're more intrigued."

The more perceptive palate combined with Parkhurst's culinary standards creates unique dining experiences. "We're making fresh pasta every day," says Dan Chiaverini, executive chef for Parkhurst Dining at Robert Morris University. "I have a person who makes pasta eight hours a day. She makes eight different sauces all week long. I have someone who breads 3,200 pieces of chicken tenders a day."

Bill Jones sums it up: "For Parkhurst, it's always been about food quality and guest service, taking care of the client, customizing per client as much as possible, being adaptive to the current trends, and trying to be ahead of that trend."

At the Root of Success

In 2001, when Parkhurst was establishing a reputation for excellence, Parkhurst chefs posed a question to the supply-chain team: Why wasn't Parkhurst buying and using more locally produced food? The chefs wanted to buy from local farms in order to feature dairy, meat, and produce sourced right in their own community.

The question was simple, but the answer was complex. Although Parkhurst units were located very close to farms, there was no established distribution infrastructure to connect with local farmers, so there was no easy way for companies like Parkhurst to purchase from local farmers. This wasn't a Parkhurst-specific problem. The buy-local concept wasn't yet embraced by grocers and restaurants, primarily because of a lack of trust between small farms and large companies – especially those that the farmers weren't familiar with.

Farmers were accustomed to selling to farm stands and directly to much smaller, independent restaurants. Parkhurst's leaders realized that they should be able to leverage the company's influence, both in the community and with their distributors, to build a supply chain infrastructure that would enable them to purchase from local farmers.

According to Jamie Moore, Parkhurst's director of sourcing and sustainability, "Small farmers weren't seeing success in the business world. I tried to let them know that I'm there to support them. I'm there to help them grow their business and expand their reach."

"In 2002, this concept of purchasing from local farmers was novel to both the farmers and local distributors," says Brooks Broadhurst. "We quickly realized that the first step, the most crucial step, was to build personal relationships with farmers – just as we were doing every day with our clients." According to Brooks, "Many of our first farmers – particularly Amish partners – were not equipped to sell to a distributor. And they were apprehensive about starting to. So we worked closely with them to address their concerns."

For instance, Parkhurst would need to adapt the company's communication channels for farmers who had technology barriers, such as no phone or internet. Farmers didn't have loading docks to accommodate the distributors' large, refrigerated vehicles. Parkhurst could make the necessary adaptations; however, there was a less tangible issue that needed to be addressed: trust.

Jamie Moore directs Parkhurst programs that support local farmers and distributors, including Dan Yarnick.

"We also guaranteed our new partners that they would be paid when they sold to our distributor," Brooks explains. "We had to show them that we would do what we promised them we would do. Most importantly, we had to put in the hard work of building relationships in order to bolster trust and create real partnerships."

Once Parkhurst addressed the farmers' concerns, the company introduced FarmSource company wide. Through the buy-local program, Parkhurst purchased 12% of its products from local partners after the first year. FarmSource grew into a guidepost for Parkhurst's purchasing strategy as the company ultimately sought to source at least 20% of its produce from local growers in season.

Since Brooks and Jamie developed the program in 2002, it has continued to evolve. In 2019, Jamie introduced an added dimension: Forged Partners. Forged Partners are purveyors of high-quality products that are produced in small quantities; products such as popcorn, salsa, beef jerky, and caramels. "They are artists and makers," Jamie explains. "They have to be family-owned or independently owned and operated. And they must be local – within 100 miles of a Parkhurst client. Our clients – as well as our chefs and our managers – have a lot of faith in the program, and they really want to help it grow."

The commitment to buying locally continues to drive the company's decision-making. FarmSource and Forged Partners help to define Parkhurst's purchasing philosophy, called "Know Your Source." Jamie explains, "Know Your Source has brought a sense of community back to our locations."

Learning for Life

Whether serving college students or corporate executives, Parkhurst chefs are in a continual learning mode. "Don't ever stop thinking you're a student," Lee Keener says. "That's one of the things I love about this business in the first place. We can learn something every single day.

"We can be as creative as we want, as long as the client approves. It's unbelievable what we're trying to do, but we're never going to stop. That's what we're here to do."

For Jeff Broadhurst, milkshakes are the perfect ending to a meal.

A Sweet Ending

From the introduction of Parkhurst Dining through today, Eat'n Park Hospitality Group continues to innovate. Going back to the earliest days of the company, the leadership never had a fear of trying new ideas, as Gas'n Glo and Eaton's prove. Another example is Park Classic Diners, which Eat'n Park introduced in Jeannette in 1999 and then expanded to Monroeville and Boardman, Ohio. The concept was designed to be the best of Eat'n Park restaurants – without the salad bar – and set in a 50s style diner. Jeff Broadhurst was a frequent guest.

"My meal was always the same when I went there," Jeff recalls. "I would order the onion rings – I can still taste them. They were just incredible. We breaded them every single day."

Following the onion rings, Jeff would order a Park Party Cake. "So, you've got this beautiful chocolate bundt cake filled with thick cream," Jeff remembers. "Then we would layer it with a chocolate fudge. Then on top of it, I would get ice cream and more fudge."

But his meal was not yet finished. "After the cake, I would get a chocolate milkshake, and that would be my meal. It was so good. Then," he says with a chuckle, "two hours later, I'd be asleep."

The diners closed in 2009. However, Jeff is still lobbying to add the Park Party Cake to the Eat'n Park menu.

Fan Favorites

What's your all-time favorite menu item?

Scott Blasey
Rock Musician and Lead Vocalist for The Clarks
"I love the baked cod at the Eat'n Park in Peters Township! I get it with a baked potato and coleslaw. Delicious and nutritious!"

Pittsburgh Dad
"Pittsburgh Dad's favorite menu item is definitely the Superburger! Coming from the city with six Super Bowl wins, it's only fitting that my choice burger get the SUPER treatment, as well!"

Larry Richert
KDKA-Radio Personality
"We never went out to eat as a family that often when I was growing up. So when we did, Eat'n Park was a treat! The Superburger was the ultimate comfort food because you really couldn't replicate it at home. Plus, French fries on the side is the perfect combo! (Fries are my kryptonite!) Ask any of my friends to this day, and they will tell you what I'll order at Eat'n Park!"

Linda Mayou
Retired Team Member
Monongahela Eat'n Park
Quarter Century Club Member
"Back in my teenage years, I would meet my boyfriend at the Whitehall Eat'n Park. My favorite meal was a Superburger, fries with gravy, and a milkshake – with two straws, of course!"

Nancy Mathews
Server, Whitehall Eat'n Park
Quarter Century Club Member
"When I was little, I'd go to my aunt's house after swim
lessons because she lived down the hill from Eat'n Park.
We'd scrape together enough money to buy a piece of
strawberry pie and then walk to the restaurant. If my mother
knew I was walking Route 51, she'd have lost her mind!"

John A. Norwig, MEd, ATC
Head Athletic Trainer
Pittsburgh Steelers
"My favorite dish from Eat'n Park is the strawberry pie. I don't feel guilty eating a
dessert that's packed full of fresh fruit!"

Rachel Petrucelli
President
UPMC Children's Hospital Foundation
"I'm a huge fan of any salad that includes fruit, but
I especially love the apple almond chicken salad at
Hello Bistro!"

Gloria Rack
50+ Year Team Member
Library Road Eat'n Park
"Rosemary chicken is my favorite. I love the sauce and great flavor. Our cooks at
Library Road cook it to perfection! I'm hoping it comes back on the menu. "

John Surma
Eat'n Park Hospitality Group
Board Member
"When I was growing up, my favorite menu item was
the Brawney Lad. Now that it's off the menu, my new
favorite is the Whale of a Cod Deluxe, chips, ranch
dressing, and slaw. Great fish, cheese, and lettuce make
it a three-course meal! Best fish sandwich ever!"

8

A Community of Caring

"Why am I doing this? You would be so much better."

With the realization that his wife was better skilled than he at making decisions about how to best support the community, Jim Broadhurst launched the new career of his wife, Suzy, as a grant maker.

The mother of three sons, a former school teacher, and a past member of the Upper St. Clair School District Board of Directors, Suzy was not intimidated by challenging work. But she didn't know how big the job was that she was stepping into. No one did.

Until the early 1990s, nonprofit organizations' requests for Eat'n Park's financial support found their way to Jim Broadhurst and Kathy James. Jim would decide the size of Eat'n Park's contribution – if any – and Kathy would write the check. As the company grew, so, too, did the requests for support.

Intrigued by the opportunity, Suzy began developing a corporate giving program in 1991. "Jim and I felt it was really important that we be community players," Suzy remembers. "We didn't want to give just to give – we wanted to be partners with people."

Jim decided that the company would dedicate 5% of pre-tax profits to corporate giving. It's a commitment the company continues today. Within that parameter, Suzy developed a structure for the company's corporate giving.

"There was never a request we received that wasn't worthy," Suzy explains. "I felt strongly that we had to have reasons to say 'yes' and reasons to say 'no.'" So she identified four broad areas of support that she believed would be important to Eat'n Park team members and guests: health and human services; culture and arts; civic affairs; and education.

"There were many ways we determined the nonprofit organizations we wanted to support," Suzy continues. "Knowing that we were always most thankful to families, children, and seniors for choosing Eat'n Park as their favorite place to eat, we wanted to support the organizations our guests relied on most."

One choice was Children's Hospital of Pittsburgh. "Every time we moved into new regions, we added the local children's hospital to our roster, wanting to ensure children and families would have access to health care," Suzy says. Another choice was United Way. "United Way helps people in their time of despair. It blankets the community and reaches more people than we can."

In addition, Eat'n Park's corporate giving always supports food banks in communities where the Restaurant Division or Parkhurst Dining has a presence. "And food banks are a natural – it's important to feed people who are hungry," she concludes.

Although Eat'n Park couldn't always provide financial support, Suzy found other means. "We could bring awareness by promoting causes to our customers," she explains. "That could be more important than money."

There was a time when Eat'n Park's support of both United Way and Women's Center & Shelter of Greater Pittsburgh unexpectedly intersected. Annually, to kick off the company's team-member campaign to support United Way, Eat'n Park invited the organization to bring a guest speaker to address a gathering of the company's general managers. One year, the speaker was a woman

who had used the services of Women's Center & Shelter.

In addressing the general managers, the speaker relayed the story of a friend whose husband was extraordinarily possessive. "She said this friend's husband didn't allow her to go anywhere by herself," Suzy relates. "He drove her to work, he picked her up after work; she wasn't allowed to have any credit cards or cash. She couldn't do anything – her husband was in total control of her life."

As the speaker described how Women's Center & Shelter helped her friend, she revealed that she was the 'friend' she was talking about. "As she concluded," Suzy remembers, "she said, 'And I worked for Eat'n Park.'"

Trina DeMarco builds on the foundation established by Suzy Broadhurst.

"It was the most shocking thing and so powerful," Suzy says. "There wasn't a dry eye in the room. And the general managers were looking at each other, realizing that this woman might have worked for them, and they never would have known what she was experiencing at home. That really connected us to United Way."

The experience created a lasting impression. With the realization that the issue of domestic abuse was one that victims tried to hide, the company placed signs in team-member break rooms with Women's Center & Shelter contact information. The signs enabled people to know help was available and gave them ways to seek it discreetly.

A short time later, the company hung posters in restaurants for guests to see. "The posters said, 'Hands are for helping, not hurting,' and gave information about how a victim of abuse could contact the shelter," Suzy explains. "We were able to reach thousands of people with the message of Women's Center & Shelter.

"Our corporate giving created a seismic shift in our general managers' understanding of the issue of domestic abuse," Suzy says. "We helped to make the issue eye opening. We helped our team members understand that it's people in our own communities who need our help. Our giving is from the heart."

Suzy and Jim's support of the community is widely known and respected. An article in PNC's 2010 *Reflections* magazine relayed, "Between them, Jim and Suzy have served on countless boards – as chairman or vice chair – including Penn State University, University of Pittsburgh, United Way of Allegheny County, Children's Hospital of Pittsburgh, The Pittsburgh Foundation, Carnegie Museums of Pittsburgh, Phipps Conservatory and the Upper St. Clair schools."

When Suzy retired in 2014, the responsibility for philanthropy was assumed by Trina DeMarco.

Team members gather before heading into the community on the Annual Day of Smiles.

Continuing the Commitment to Community

Suzy had established a solid baseline for how to continue the important work that was aligned with one of the company's core values: We care about people. "The spirit of philanthropy grew very organically," Trina DeMarco explains. However, as the geographic footprint of the company expanded, the challenge became how to continue the authentic commitment to community in areas that, in some cases, are thousands of miles from the company's Corporate Support Center.

The answer is a bit cliché, but true: company leadership not only talks the talk, they also walk the walk. And team members follow in their footsteps.

To build understanding of how community commitment is driven by team members, regardless of where they work within the Hospitality Group, the company relies on storytelling through a combination of newsletters, posters, and other internal channels.

"We want to bring visibility and use this incredible work as a point of pride because it's really something our team members should be – and are – proud of," Trina explains. "Being in the hospitality industry, we love taking care of people. We love serving people, so it's not surprising that our people are passionate about extending that care."

And that's where volunteerism comes in. "We create teams of volunteers in support of our corporate-giving focus, and they are often based on team members' passions," Trina continues. "Instead of only talking about our support of food banks, for instance, we sign up a group of team members to volunteer at a local food bank."

It's a strategy with multiple benefits. The local organizations receive support, and team members learn about their neighbors in the communities they serve.

Team members participate in volunteer opportunities throughout the year. The opportunities range from large events, like the City of Pittsburgh Great Race, to community projects, like the Annual Day of Smiles – a company-wide initiative when team members volunteer at nonprofit organizations throughout Pittsburgh and in neighborhoods where Eat'n Park restaurants and Parkhurst accounts are located. "Team members grow to understand the work that our partners are doing," Trina says.

Team members throughout the entire Hospitality Group are encouraged to pursue volunteerism in other aspects of their life, too. To support their interests, the company recognizes team members each year through the Volunteer of the Year program. Team members can nominate co-workers who they believe demonstrate an extraordinary commitment to volunteerism in their personal lives. The field of nominees is narrowed to finalists. A panel of outside judges determines the Volunteer of the Year, and Eat'n Park Hospitality Group contributes $1,000 to the individual's charity of choice. The company also contributes smaller amounts to the charities of choice of each of the finalists.

"Our philanthropy is always evolving," Trina concludes. "That's the only way to affect positive change. We monitor what's happening in the community and adapt to support that."

Caring for Kids: Igniting a Movement

Throughout the years at Eat'n Park, there have been many sparks – individuals whose efforts ignite meaningful, lasting efforts. There is no better example than the Caring for Kids Campaign that benefits children's hospitals in the communities where Eat'n Park Hospitality Group has a presence.

It was Christmastime 1978, and Kay Neely was a cook at the Butler Eat'n Park restaurant. She had heard that KDKA-Radio was raising funds for Children's Hospital of Pittsburgh. She and her colleagues decided to participate in the fundraising.

"They decided to go Christmas caroling up and down the main road where the restaurant is located," explains Trina DeMarco. "They cut slits in cottage cheese containers, and that was their vessel for collecting funds. In one evening, they raised several hundred dollars."

Kay gathered the money and headed to downtown Pittsburgh. She planned to announce the donation on KDKA-Radio's live broadcast. But there was one thing she needed to do first.

"She called Jim Broadhurst and told him to turn on the radio," Trina relates. "When Kay presented the cash from the guests and neighbors of the Butler Eat'n Park, she threw down a challenge: 'If our little restaurant can raise this money, what about the other restaurants?'"

Jim Broadhurst was listening. The next year he sent Kay a letter accepting her challenge, and 1979 became the first year of company-wide fundraising for Children's Hospital of Pittsburgh.

Jim formalized the fundraising effort, designating a timeframe from mid-November through mid-December and establishing a process for raising money for the Free Care Fund at Children's Hospital of Pittsburgh.

Jim wanted the Eat'n Park campaign to be a very local one. Each restaurant would conduct their own fundraising. Ideas were plentiful – traditional ideas, like street collecting, bake sales, and bingo; and less traditional ideas, like Bop til You Drop – an oldies dance; Round Up – an opportunity for guests to round up their bill to the next dollar amount, donating the extra change to the campaign; and even a rooftop campaign.

Suzy and Jim embraced the campaign as a family opportunity. "It was all about having fun while raising money to achieve a successful campaign for the kids at Children's Hospital," Suzy explains. "When they were young, our boys loved collecting donations at busy intersections and competing to see who could raise the most money. But stopping cars in traffic was determined to be a little too dangerous," she says with a chuckle, "so the practice was stopped."

Kay Neely and colleagues from the Butler Eat'n
Park count money raised from caroling in 1978.

December 26, 1979

Ms. Mary Kay Neely
53 Old Plank Road
Butler, PA 16001

Dear Ms. Neely,

        We didn't forget your challenge to the other
Eat'n Park restaurants to share in the joy and
happiness from raising money for Children's Hospital.
You personally deserve to be proud of your efforts
toward the success of our campaign, as a result of
your input. We're proud and grateful to have people
like you at Eat'n Park.

        Thank you and best wishes for a healthful and
happy New Year.

                        Sincerely,

                        James S. Broadhurst
                        President

JSB/kak

Letter to Kay from Jim Broadhurst recognizing her for inspiring the first official
company-wide campaign, following her 1978 effort

"This is a grassroots, team-member-driven campaign," Trina stresses. "It is supported by some company infrastructure, but team-member passion has driven it since 1979."

"The campaign energizes our guests," Suzy adds. "They do more than just support the campaign; they become engaged in it. Because of their generosity, Eat'n Park has become known for supporting our communities where we do business."

The first year of the campaign, Eat'n Park raised $47,000. Each subsequent year, restaurant team members and guests raised more and more money. In 1987, the Eat'n Park campaign reached a milestone, raising $1 million since its inception.

Now called *Caring for Kids*, the campaign has such community support that Eat'n Park has gone on to become one of the top fundraisers for the Free Care Fund at UPMC Children's Hospital of Pittsburgh, raising more than $8 million through 2021.

"The initiative gives us the opportunity to give back and support guests and team members who have needed the best medical care for their children and grandchildren," Suzy explains. Guests have been so good to us over the years," she continues, "and we all want to give back through our philanthropic efforts to support their greatest needs."

In 1992, Eat'n Park moved beyond western Pennsylvania and entered the central Pennsylvania, West Virginia, and eastern Ohio markets. And the Caring for Kids campaign followed with its emphasis on local communities.

When Eat'n Park Hospitality Group introduced Parkhurst Dining in 1996, the commitment to local communities continued. With locations outside of western Pennsylvania, early clients Highmark and PNC took Parkhurst into new markets, including Camp Hill, Pennsylvania, and Grand Rapids, Michigan. Again, the Caring for Kids campaign followed.

Kay Neely returned to the area to visit the new Butler restaurant in 2021.

As the geographic footprint has grown, Eat'n Park Restaurants and Parkhurst Dining have added more children's hospitals to the list of beneficiaries, always keeping the funds in the local community. The Caring for Kids Campaign has raised more than $11 million for all children's hospitals in the company's service areas.

"The premise of the campaign that we're really passionate about is that the money that our team members raise stays in their local community," Trina explains. "We are obsessive about that."

Kay Neely never could have envisioned that her simple – yet innovative – idea would evolve into a multistate campaign with in-person and online initiatives. And she likely never imagined that the campaign would raise more than $11 million to provide free medical care to children whose families could not otherwise afford to pay for it. Her spark ignited a fire – tended and cared for by team members ever since – that has warmed the hearts of many.

***

In Tune

Fundraising for the Caring for Kids Campaign takes many forms. There have always been bake sales, raffles, and various contests. But one fundraising idea followed a harmonious path.

"I was driving past the Squirrel Hill restaurant," Jim Broadhurst remembers. "It was during the holiday season in 1981, and there were two women standing in front of our restaurant singing Christmas carols. I was fascinated."

Jim parked his car and walked over to the women, asking where they were from and if they worked for the restaurant. Sally Mace and Carolyn Valentine told him they were servers at Eat'n Park, and they both were studying music at Carnegie Mellon University.

Sally Mace led the Eat'n Park Singers as they spread holiday joy throughout the community.

"It immediately occurred to me – we have two people in one restaurant who are great singers, and they are singing Christmas carols," Jim relates. "With as many team members as we had – we probably had several thousand by then – we had to have the nucleus to have a really good choir. We could send people out during the holiday season to sing at nursing homes and different places and raise money for Children's Hospital.

"Kathy James was the production manager and scheduler for the singers," Jim continues. "It was a job with no pay, and her night job included helping ensure that the singers and equipment arrived on time."

"I couldn't carry a tune," Kathy quips, "but I could carry equipment!"

In 1982, the singers went on the road. They rented a coach bus and traveled from one Eat'n Park restaurant to another to sing Christmas carols for guests. To conclude their first season, the singers traveled to Children's Hospital to perform for the patients.

With the second year of the Eat'n Park Singers approaching, the group had an idea – record a Christmas album. Sally Mace arranged to use space at the Mellon Institute near Carnegie Mellon University to record the album.

"I don't know how many albums we sold, but we raised a lot of money for Children's Hospital," Jim says.

The singers were becoming a popular entertainment group, and requests for their talents began to extend beyond the restaurants, including Phipps Conservatory and Botanical Gardens and the 1983 Kaufmann's Christmas Parade.

The highlight for the singers may have been an invitation to perform with The Pittsburgh Ballet Theatre in its presentation of Tchaikovsky's "The Nutcracker."

An article in Eat'n Park's internal newsletter proclaimed: *"Their first performance at Heinz Hall was such a success that "The Nutcracker's" Maestro DeRosa insisted that they perform nightly. Before the final evening's ballet, the Singers performed on the second balcony level in the lobby and the applause was especially exuberant from the crowded gathering of Heinz Hall patrons as Miss Valentine concluded her solo, 'O Holy Night.'"*

Carolyn Valentine who, at the time, was a service supervisor at the Squirrel Hill Eat'n Park, was quoted in the article, saying: *"The accolades we received were especially meaningful because the Singers exist for one main reason – to help the kids at Children's Hospital."*

A Moving Idea

In 1991, one idea set in motion a new method of raising funds for the Caring for Kids campaign. Dennis Quinlisk, who at the time was the general manager of the Whitehall Eat'n Park, had an idea. He thought that the campaign would get a big boost if they could raffle something major, something that everyone could use. It was perfectly clear to Dennis that they needed to introduce a car raffle. There was one small detail to consider: they would need a brand-new car.

A problem solver by nature, Dennis knew of only one way to secure a new car for the campaign – buy it. So, unbeknownst to his family, Dennis took out a second mortgage on his home. He used the money to buy a big, new Pontiac Bonneville, which he promptly donated to Eat'n Park.

Dennis coerced his friend and colleague Don Micheals into joining him in the escapade. Don was the manager at the Natrona Heights restaurant.

Dennis and Don purchased 400 Pennsylvania Lottery tickets. The restaurants sold the tickets as part of their fundraising campaign, and that first year, team members sold all but 40 tickets. What if the winning ticket was among the ones not sold? Jim Broadhurst wasn't going to let that be an issue – he bought all the remaining 40 tickets and put the names of others on them.

The car raffle idea worked – that year, the campaign raised $40,000 more than the previous year's campaign. The car raffle has continued ever since. Fortunately, Dennis hasn't had to buy a new car every year. Lincoln Mercury dealers were the first to donate a vehicle every year to be raffled, with proceeds benefitting the Free Care Fund. The tradition is now continued through the generosity of Neighborhood Ford Store.

The scheme Dennis Quinlisk and Don Micheals concocted led to an annual car raffle as an essential element in the company's Caring for Kids fundraising campaigns.

A Classic Thank You

Eat'n Park Hospitality Group has been inextricably tied to community support since Jim Broadhurst joined Eat'n Park Restaurants in 1973. Through team-member-supported campaigns like United Way and Caring for Kids, the company has helped to raise millions of dollars for local organizations.

In 1982, on the eve of launching the Caring for Kids campaign to benefit local children's hospitals, Jim was inspired. "I wanted to make a holiday commercial as a way of thanking the community. I didn't want to promote Eat'n Park; I simply wanted to express our appreciation."

That desire gave birth to what has become known as the "Christmas Star commercial."

Jim asked Eat'n Park's advertising agency at the time, Ketchum McLeod & Grove, to create a video Christmas card to demonstrate gratitude for the community's support. It was a low-budget project, so the agency assigned it to a young, less expensive team: Craig Otto, an art director, and Cathy Bowen, a young copywriter.

Three weeks and many stalled ideas later, Craig and Cathy decided to explore an animated approach. Craig was in his office one Sunday and began sketching a star. "How does the star get to the top of the Christmas tree?" he asked himself. As he continued to sketch ideas, he hit upon the tree helping the star. Coincidentally, Cathy also was in the office that Sunday, working on a simple message to accompany the animation.

The concept was exactly what Jim wanted: a message for the community that begins simply with a tiny star struggling to reach the top of a Christmas tree. The tree bends down to lift the star to the top, and the star and tree burst into color once the star is in place.

"We like to say Eat'n Park is the place for smiles, and for decades, the Christmas Star commercial has been bringing a smile to the face of people throughout the Pittsburgh community and, now, throughout the world."

The original script was equally simple and poignant: *We hope the lift you get this holiday season lasts the whole year through. Merry Christmas from Eat'n Park.*

With Jim's approval gained, the Ketchum team worked with specialists to finish production of the commercial. According to a *Pittsburgh Post-Gazette* article, Ovation Films, based in New York City, hand-drew 720 acetate cells that became the animation. The lead animator on the project was Nancy Beiman, a freelancer. Walt Woodward from Perfect Pitch in Cleveland wrote the score, and Bob Trow, a Pittsburgh radio and TV personality, provided the voiceover.

The Christmas Star Commercial has survived the test of time to become a classic.

Each year, the Christmas Star commercial begins airing on Thanksgiving Day during the Macy's Thanksgiving Day Parade. Many consider the commercial to signify the beginning of the Christmas season. Thanks to YouTube, Facebook, and various other Internet sites and social media platforms, the commercial has an international following. People can view it on their TV, computer, tablet, cell phone, and smart watch. To cut down on phone calls to the restaurants, Eat'n Park annually lists the air dates of the commercial on its website (www.eatnpark.com).

"The Christmas tree bending down to give the star a lift is symbolic of the spirit of Pittsburghers. Pittsburghers have a history of giving a lift to others," Jim says. "We like to say Eat'n Park is the place for smiles and, for decades, the Christmas Star commercial has been bringing a smile to the face of people throughout the Pittsburgh community and now, throughout the world."

9

Smiley
From Sweet Cookie to Superstar Icon

When Jim Broadhurst was growing up in 1949 in Titusville, Pennsylvania, he walked to and from school every day. On his way home, he stopped at Warner's Bakery and bought a cookie – a small, round, sugar cookie. And against the cookie's white icing, the bakers drew a colorful smiley face. "I bought so many cookies, my friends started calling me 'Cookie,'" Jim laughs.

That small cookie became a big idea in 1986 when Eat'n Park Restaurants introduced the Smiley Cookie. Jim thought the cookie he loved as a kid would make a nice treat for young guests at Eat'n Park. The restaurants were introducing bakeries with pies, sticky buns, and Boston brown bread, and the cookies could be baked and decorated inhouse. "We sent a team member to apprentice with Warner's Bakery," Jim recalls. "They taught her exactly how to make the cookie." With that knowledge, Eat'n Park began baking Smiley Cookies, and all young diners at the end of their meal were given a cookie decorated with green eyes, a nose, and a smile.

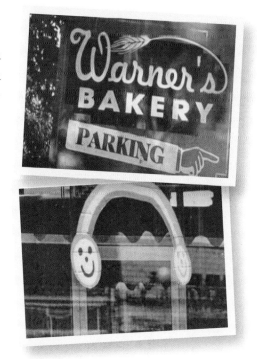

Initially, the Smiley Cookie had its detractors. Some team members thought the cookie was too big and too sweet. But Jim held firm in wanting to recreate the cookie from his youth: "No. This is what it is. It's a large, sweet cookie for children. They love it big, and big is memorable, and that's the way it should be."

"I was a server then," remembers Mercy Senchur, chief operating officer of Eat'n Park's Restaurant Division, "and as soon as I would give the cookie to a child, the parent would say, 'Can I buy one of those?'" But they weren't for sale; they were only for the kids.

As more adults expressed an interest in buying Smiley Cookies, Basil Cox, then president of Eat'n Park Restaurants, knew they needed to respond to consumer demand. "We had to figure out how to charge for them, how to package them. Once we got over those hurdles, we had to start thinking about ways to display them in the restaurants."

A Menu of Ideas

Pittsburgh advertising agency HBM/Creamer represented Eat'n Park in 1990. One day, Cliff Miller, creative director at Creamer at the time, had a lunch meeting with Basil Cox. As Cliff looked over the menu at the Robinson Township Eat'n Park, he noticed something in small type: "Free Smiley Cookie for kids 12 and under."

"Bingo!" Cliff remembers saying to Basil. "I'm going to make Smiley famous. This is your advertising critter, and you don't even know it. He could be your Mickey Mouse."

When Cliff looked at the Smiley Cookie, he saw beyond the happy, round face; he saw a brand. In the months that followed, Cliff introduced Smiley on all Eat'n Park materials. The first project was a three-sided table tent promoting breakfast, and it showed Smiley peeking around the corner. "It had nothing to do with breakfast," Cliff remembers. "It had everything to do with brand."

"The big jump was to think, 'OK, this is more than a cookie," Basil remembers. "This can be a symbol of Eat'n Park. It can have many applications, and it can be seen in many different ways. That conjunction of the symbol and the cookie and the experience is a very important one."

Soon, Smiley began popping up everywhere. "Smiley represents the Eat'n Park culture," Cliff explains. "We've always wanted to do things that make people smile – our guests, our team members, our neighbors."

One year after beginning to position Smiley as a brand icon – and with a smiling cookie looking over his shoulder – Cliff introduced a new tagline and jingle: "Eat'n Park's the place for smiles."

"It became the personality of Eat'n Park," remembers Basil. "It ended up giving Eat'n Park its basic identity – The Place for Smiles. That's powerful."

the place for Smiles™

Smiley on the Move

It was August 1992, and Cliff had an idea: bring Smiley to life through a commercial produced in claymation, a form of animation. The technique had been popularized in the mid-1980s through a commercial for California Raisins.

Cliff's idea required that Smiley would be created from clay, positioned, then photographed. Each slight move of Smiley would require repositioning the clay creation and photographing it. Then, 24 images would be projected each second. And there would be no opportunity for editing.

"I had already spent my entire production budget at that point," Cliff explains. "But when I pitched the idea to Basil, he loved it." So, Cliff contacted the California agency that created the California Raisins and gave them a new project.

"The ad said simply, 'Smiley Cookies to go!' It started airing in Pittsburgh on a Monday. By Wednesday, the restaurants sold out of cookies."

Smiley Cookies quickly became popular in the restaurants with guests purchasing them by the dozen. Eventually, Cliff broke the mold of the original Smiley Cookies with green icing. Cookies began taking a variety of shapes and colors. Eat'n Park introduced Smiley Cookies that were coordinated with the time of year – red hearts for Valentine's Day, green shamrocks for St. Patrick's Day, pastel flowers in the springtime, and orange jack-o-lanterns at Halloween.

Smiley Comes to Life

In 1997, Cliff had the opportunity to transition from managing Eat'n Park's creative at the company's advertising agency to joining Eat'n Park as the company's vice president of creative services. Cliff seized the opportunity. Under his creative leadership, Smiley began to transform from a cookie to an icon.

It didn't take long for Smiley to be gracing merchandise, including mugs, t-shirts, key chains, and more. The more Smiley was seen, the greater the demand.

Internationally acclaimed artist Burton Morris showed his hometown pride by celebrating Smiley's 25th birthday with a painting of everyone's favorite cookie.

Cliff realized it was time for Eat'n Park to give birth to Smiley as an actual, tangible mascot. With arms and legs and a smile from ear to ear, Smiley quickly was embraced – literally and figuratively – by kids and adults alike. Kevin O'Connell, Eat'n Park's senior vice president of marketing at the time, says, "I really wanted to set Disney as the standard for what a person's experience with this character should be; there's a mystery to it, there's a magic."

To transport Smiley to public appearances, Eat'n Park created the Cookie Cruiser in 2004. Getting Smiley to the right place at the right time required assistance – Team Smiley to the rescue. The team began as a summer internship program with two college students. It grew gradually, reaching six students in 2019. To make the team, members must graduate from Smiley University, a training program for learning all things Smiley. Team Smiley accompanies Smiley on about 150 appearances every year.

Smiley's Big Score

Smiley leaped to national status in 2006 when the Pittsburgh Steelers went to Super Bowl® XL to face the Seattle Seahawks. "We knew this was going to be a big deal for Smiley Cookies," Kevin O'Connell relates. "We got Pittsburgh Mayor O'Connor and Pennsylvania Governor Rendell to include Smiley Cookies in the bets against their Seattle counterparts. It generated a lot of publicity."

It also generated a lot of interest in Smiley Cookies. "Literally, people were making cookies 24/7 at the restaurants," Kevin laughs. "We could not keep up with demand. As fast as they'd put a box out, somebody would buy it. It was one of the most amazing and stressful experiences. You have a product that everyone wants, and if you could only make them faster, you could sell more. But that was pretty legendary in the company at the time."

Sales weren't limited to the restaurants, though. Eat'n Park quietly had been making Smiley Cookies available through the restaurants' website. They decided to make a little more noise about ordering cookies online.

"We started small with the e-commerce initiative," Brooks Broadhurst remembers. But with the Steelers going to the Super Bowl, they saw an opportunity. "We offered free shipping to the state of Washington since the Steelers were playing the Seattle Seahawks. It was costly," Brooks says, "but it jump-started our online sales." That week, 350,000 Smiley Cookies made their way to Steelers fans throughout the country.

To accommodate the growth of online cookie sales, Eat'n Park created a more robust, dedicated website with an easy-to-remember address: www.SmileyCookie.com. The e-commerce team worked with consultants to develop a customized software product. They had thought of everything, including all possible color combinations and all possible mailing needs.

The other new tool was the Cookie Factory, a bakery and distribution center exclusively focused on Smiley Cookies. The Cookie Factory provided expanded capacity to handle increased demand. Here, team members could mix, cut, bake, decorate, package, and ship cookies to fulfill orders placed through SmileyCookie.com.

So in 2009, when the Steelers were headed to Super Bowl XLIII in Tampa, Eat'n Park was certain they could meet the anticipated heightened demand for Smiley Cookies. SmileyCookie.com was primed, the Cookie Factory was equipped and staffed, and everyone was ready for an influx of orders.

That is, until the website crashed.

"It was a disaster of epic proportions," Brooks says, now able to chuckle about it. The new software enabled people to order Smiley Cookies, but when orders totaled more than 500,000 cookies, it triggered a glitch in the programming, and not all the orders were able to be filled. "We couldn't ship," Brooks explains. "We had about a 20% failure rate."

Although not everyone had their cookies in time for the big game, Eat'n Park followed up with the disappointed fans by shipping cookies at a later date and refunding their money.

Looking back on the experience now, Brooks says, "It was a successful failure. We sold lots of cookies and had lots of happy customers. And," he says, "it gave another bump to our e-commerce."

When the Steelers returned to the Super Bowl in 2011, all systems – human, mechanical, and technological – had no difficulty fulfilling the demand for 600,000 Smiley Cookies.

Today, the Cookie Factory produces all Smiley Cookies ordered through the dedicated website. The factory is staffed by 10-20 team members, depending on the season. In 2021, the smile makers at the Cookie Factory produced and shipped 11 million Smiley Cookies!

Ambassador Smiley

Nancy Mathews, a long-time server at the Whitehall Eat'n Park, discovered first-hand the widespread power of Smiley Cookies. She and her husband, Tom – general manager at the Belle Vernon Eat'n Park at the time – were planning a trip to Washington, D.C., with their daughters. They contacted the office of Mike Doyle, their Congressional representative, and the staff sent the Mathews family tourist information about Washington.

"So, I said to my husband, 'We're going to go to his office, and we're going to take these Smiley Cookies to them for sending us the information.'" When Nancy got to his office, she said to the staff, "I just wanted to bring these to you because you sent us such useful information." The staff was thrilled. "Cookies from home!"

They asked Nancy if there was anything they could do while she and her family were in D.C. Nancy politely asked, "You wouldn't happen to have any White House tour tickets, would you?" The staff explained that they already had distributed their allocation of tickets. Disappointed but understanding, Nancy continued small talk with the staff – where they were staying, what they were planning to see, the age of the Mathews girls.

"By the time we got back to our hotel," Nancy remembers, "there was a phone call saying, 'We have tour tickets for you.' They sent them to our hotel, and we got to take the White House tour. Smiley Cookies are the best ambassador."

An Iconic Smile

Over several decades, the cookies with a smiling face went from being a boyhood treat to an internationally known icon of Eat'n Park Restaurants. So, what's the secret to the success of Smiley? Cliff explains it simply: "Smiley creates smiles, makes people smile, makes people feel good, and makes people happy. That's why he's the identity for the brand. It's the power of Smiley."

Cliff Miller saw the potential power of Smiley.

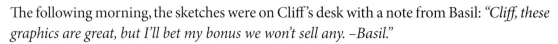

Hooked on Smiley Cookies

In July 2005, Pittsburgh was hosting the Bassmaster Classic, considered by fishing aficionados to be the Super Bowl of bass fishing. Cliff Miller, an avid fisherman, started sketching fish-shaped Smiley Cookies and materials to support them – mobiles, window posters, table tent cards. Cliff took the sketches to Basil Cox and laid them on his desk with a note: *"Basil, these are my graphic elements to promote the fish cookie. We have to do the fish cookie this year. This bass fishing tournament is going to be a big deal. We could have the cookies in restaurants the beginning of July, and on July 31st, it ends. But there's going to be all this talk about fishing in Pittsburgh."*

"I never understood it," Basil Cox remembers. "A fish cookie? It doesn't make any sense."

The following morning, the sketches were on Cliff's desk with a note from Basil: *"Cliff, these graphics are great, but I'll bet my bonus we won't sell any. –Basil."*

Following the Bassmaster Classic, Basil made an announcement at a monthly leadership meeting: "We sold all those fish cookies. It's the best-selling cookie we ever had. They even beat Valentine's Day in sales. And I didn't want to do it, but Cliff insisted."

Cliff sat at the table, smugly waving a yellow note. Jim Broadhurst asked him what he was doing. "I read the note from Basil verbatim," Cliff remembers. "It ended with, 'I'll bet my bonus.' Everyone laughed. But I never saw a penny of his bonus!" Cliff says with a chuckle.

Cliff Miller had a seemingly endless supply of creative ideas, and one of them was designed to lift spirits – a Smiley hot air balloon. The balloon launched in 1994 and sailed above regattas, arts festivals, and community celebrations. Smiley continued to fly for seven years. The hot air balloon industry took a marked decline after events of September 11, 2001, and never fully recovered. Smiley the balloon was grounded but hopes for the icon continued to sail high.

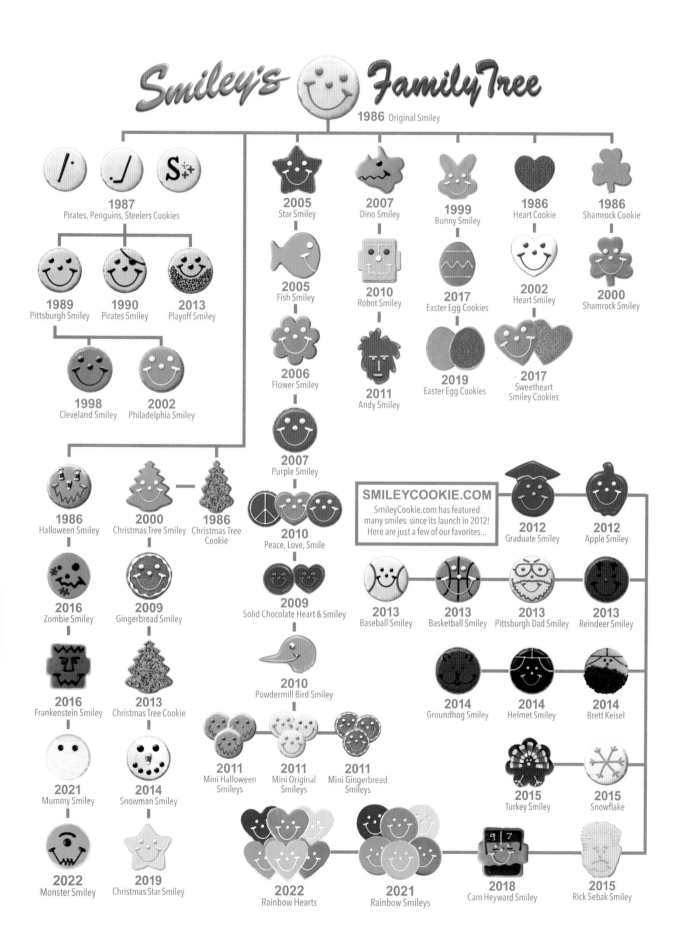

Smiley's Family Tree

1986 Original Smiley

1987
Pirates, Penguins, Steelers Cookies

1989
Pittsburgh Smiley

1990
Pirates Smiley

2013
Playoff Smiley

1998
Cleveland Smiley

2002
Philadelphia Smiley

2005
Star Smiley

2005
Fish Smiley

2006
Flower Smiley

2007
Purple Smiley

2010
Peace, Love, Smile

2009
Solid Chocolate Heart & Smiley

2010
Powdermill Bird Smiley

2011
Mini Halloween Smileys

2011
Mini Original Smileys

2011
Mini Gingerbread Smileys

2007
Dino Smiley

2010
Robot Smiley

2011
Andy Smiley

1999
Bunny Smiley

2017
Easter Egg Cookies

2019
Easter Egg Cookies

1986
Heart Cookie

2002
Heart Smiley

2017
Sweetheart Smiley Cookies

1986
Shamrock Cookie

2000
Shamrock Smiley

1986
Halloween Smiley

2000
Christmas Tree Smiley

1986
Christmas Tree Cookie

2016
Zombie Smiley

2009
Gingerbread Smiley

2016
Frankenstein Smiley

2013
Christmas Tree Cookie

2021
Mummy Smiley

2014
Snowman Smiley

2022
Monster Smiley

2019
Christmas Star Smiley

2022
Rainbow Hearts

2021
Rainbow Smileys

2018
Cam Heyward Smiley

2015
Rick Sebak Smiley

SMILEYCOOKIE.COM
SmileyCookie.com has featured many smiles since its launch in 2012! Here are just a few of our favorites...

2012
Graduate Smiley

2012
Apple Smiley

2013
Baseball Smiley

2013
Basketball Smiley

2013
Pittsburgh Dad Smiley

2013
Reindeer Smiley

2014
Groundhog Smiley

2014
Helmet Smiley

2014
Brett Keisel

2015
Turkey Smiley

2015
Snowflake

10

Innovation and Compassion
The North Star for
Navigating a Pandemic

The year 2020 dawned with great promise. With a nod toward the standard for perfect vision, individuals and companies looked at the new year as an opportunity to see things with clarity.

No one counted on a pandemic.

A term that few people were familiar with on the first day of the new year was part of daily conversations long before the final day of the year: COVID-19. It quickly made its way around the world. On March 11, 2020, the World Health Organization declared COVID a pandemic. Terms like, "social distancing," "incubation period," "flattening the curve," and "herd immunity" were routinely uttered, and frequently, done so behind a face mask.

As scientists around the world worked to develop a vaccine, seemingly every aspect of life changed profoundly – going to work or school, visiting with friends and family, traveling to favorite vacation destinations…and eating at restaurants.

The pandemic spared no industry; however, it decimated the tourism and hospitality industries. Eat'n Park Hospitality Group managed the pandemic with innovation and compassion, finding different ways to create smiles for as many people as possible, including the team members the company was forced to furlough.

"We had two objectives for getting through the pandemic," Jeff Broadhurst explains. "First, take care of our team members, and second, save our company."

Innovation: Anticipation

At the time of the pandemic, the Restaurant Division and Parkhurst Dining had a presence in 13 different states, and different counties in each state frequently changed mandates for restaurants, food service, colleges, universities, and employers – often with very little notice. At various times, mandates ranged from full closure to 50% capacity to full capacity; from masks being required to being requested to being unnecessary. To manage a nearly unmanageable environment, Eat'n Park Hospitality Group relied on well-developed plans and innovative solutions.

Bill Moore didn't simply respond to crises, he anticipated them.

"The foresight of the company – starting with the core values – really set us up for how to handle the pandemic," says Bill Moore, the company's retired director of safety and security. Bill's job was not simply to respond to crises, but to anticipate them and prepare. Although COVID was unknown to many, Bill had developed a pandemic plan a decade earlier that became a guide for managing the COVID outbreak

Also dating back a decade or so was the introduction of pickup windows at Eat'n Park restaurants. In 2008, the Monroeville restaurant opened the door to a new way of serving guests – ordering by phone for picking up at a designated window on the side of the restaurant (ordering online and through the Eat'n Park app followed a few years later). Guests could pick up their meal without entering the restaurant, then enjoy it in the comfort of their home. The company was one of the first sit-down restaurants in the region to implement pickup windows and introduced them at as many restaurants as possible over the following years. In 2008, pickup windows were innovative; in 2020, pickup windows were essential.

"The foresight of the company, starting with the core values, really set us up for how to handle the pandemic."

— Bill Moore

Innovation: Acceleration and Adaptation

Rich Liebscher ensured the company's technology was scalable in the event of a crisis.

Technology innovations also positioned the Hospitality Group to better serve guests and clients. Rich Liebscher, senior vice president, corporate development, and chief information officer, oversaw the application and adaptation of technology. "From a technology perspective, we really were in a good position because of previous investments," he explains. "We had a very scalable digital ordering system in place; we had already explored delivery concepts. And, so, it was a case of, 'Can we scale them all quickly?'"

In a typical environment, Eat'n Park will test a concept at a handful of restaurants. If it is working well, the process will be re-evaluated before determining if it should be implemented across the Restaurant Division. "In this environment, we had to make go/no-go decisions in a week or so as we encountered changing regulations from counties and states," Rich says. "This 70-year-old company was able to pivot much more quickly than it did in the past."

A decision that needed to be made quickly was how to adapt the extensive Eat'n Park menu for a take-out only operation. What are the favorites? What will travel well? What is easy for team members to prepare?

One of the more challenging considerations: What was available?

"One of the things that we found is that manufacturers would eliminate big parts of their offerings," explains Dave Beauvais, vice president, supply chain. That meant that he and his team needed to identify options that were comparable in price, exact in flavor, and available.

"We would make that determination in the space of an afternoon because the clock was ticking," Dave says. "We were thinking, 'We're going to run out in two months. We've got to solve this problem right now.' So, we cut a whole bunch of red tape because we had to."

When supply chain issues developed, Dave Beauvais needed to find solutions.

The company also introduced different processes for getting meals to guests, including delivery services, lobby pickup shelves, and curbside service, wherever possible. "All of those programs had been tried over the last two years," Rich explains. "The system we had in place for digital ordering and online ordering helped us to scale that."

At Parkhurst Dining, reality was just as challenging. Every client – whether college or corporation – was making decisions regarding staying open, being fully virtual, or some version of hybrid. Parkhurst needed to be ready to respond quickly and flexibly to each client's decisions. Again, innovation paved the way.

"We rapidly scaled mobile ordering for the higher education accounts," Rich explains. "Amazingly, with the younger demographic, as much as they enjoy mobile, it didn't have much traction pre-pandemic. It was always just so convenient to walk outside your dorm, and there's a food court steps away."

COVID changed that overnight. "Meals had to be either delivered to the dorm or picked up in a manner similar to what we were doing in the restaurants," says Rich. "It's a tale of innovation, but also of agility and a digital-fast mindset."

Those attributes – agility and a digital-fast mindset – apply to how the company serves guests and clients. But Eat'n Park Hospitality Group also needed to keep its operations running smoothly as an employer.

"We were an early adopter of technology," Rich explains. "We partnered with Zoom and Microsoft Teams years before. Even though the company is driven by personal relationships, communication really picked up during the pandemic. The flow of information and feedback sped up."

Not only did the company already have technology in place for meetings and training, it also had technology in place for other operations. "We had a lot of cloud platforms. Our whole payroll system could be managed remotely. Our human resources team could work from anywhere. That was all in place."

There is always some risk with innovation. It's an expensive investment, and it may not live up to expectations. Rich credits the executive team and the company's Board of Directors for being willing to make the investment. The company had already moved through a digital transformation, so they didn't lose time determining how to build and implement new systems.

"We already had gotten the technology to everyone, trained them, leveraged it, and tweaked it for the business. We were in a really good position," Rich says.

Many of the processes that were utilized during the pandemic likely will remain in place for normal, day-to-day operations. Rich foresees that pay-at-table devices and QR codes for self-checkout may become standard features.

Eat'n Park Hospitality Group plans to continue investing in innovative solutions. "We need to continue to pivot and adapt as the needs and wants and environment evolve," Rich explains. "No matter how you choose to interact with us, our future is to continue to make that experience as convenient as possible. If a guest is dining in one of our restaurants or in a corporate or college cafeteria, we want to ensure that the experience is convenient and easy to use."

Eat'n Park Hospitality Group always made safety a top priority, and its importance only increased during the pandemic. Once regulations changed and as people were returning to dining in restaurants and cafeterias, both the Restaurant Division and Parkhurst wanted to ensure that guests and clients felt comfortable with the safety measures in place.

"Safety was at the forefront of our discussions," Rich notes. "What are we doing for guests? For team members? What are we doing from a regulatory perspective to make sure that we're not only in compliance, but above compliance? We want that to live on, whether you are dining at a Parkhurst location or one of our restaurants."

"Thank goodness Eat'n Park Hospitality Group had the foresight to make a lot of bold movements before the pandemic," Bill Moore reflects. "The pandemic was a little bit of everything – nightmare, frustration, satisfaction – but it was a lot of growth."

Innovation: Compassion and Community

In March 2020, several business leaders gathered to discuss how COVID was affecting the community. Bill Demchak, chairman, president, and chief executive officer; and Greg Jordan, executive vice president, general counsel and chief administrative officer, both of The PNC Financial Services Group, mentioned to Jeff Broadhurst that, since the closure of schools curtailed a food source for many students, they wanted PNC to make an investment that would alleviate that problem.

Jeff tapped his brother Brooks and representatives from United Way of Southwestern Pennsylvania to join the PNC Foundation to work out a solution. PNC was willing to invest $1 million to support the community. Brooks suggested that PNC contribute the funds to United Way so that the organization could manage the programmatic details and raise additional funding while Eat'n

Park Hospitality Group coordinated all aspects of food, from sourcing to developing menus to preparing and delivering.

Just as the community leaders were finalizing logistics, a representative from Duquesne City School District called. The district's food service provider stopped meal service due to COVID exposures in the kitchen. "We were able to step in when they called and just started making bag lunches," Brooks explains. "And then things took off."

The entire operation ran as smoothly as if it were long-standing. Duquesne City School District paid their school bus provider to deliver an agreed-upon number of lunches at scheduled stops. The district informed parents of the time the school bus would arrive at their stop so that they could meet the bus and pick up the meals. Initially, Eat'n Park delivered the meals to the buses. Eventually, the buses went to the Homestead restaurant to pick up the lunches.

Similar processes were set up through Access and school districts to deliver meals to Penn Hills, McKees Rocks, and the Mon Valley. Brooks explains, "Carnegie Mellon mapped out the routes for the buses based on community need."

As funding grew from donors and the government, the scope of the school program also grew. "We were operating on a shoestring," Brooks explains. The burgeoning operation ended up serving 16 school districts, north to Butler, south to Uniontown, east to Jeannette and Latrobe, and throughout Allegheny County.

"We started with bagged lunches because that was what was needed at the time," Brooks explains. "Then we started providing lunches for Allegheny County Housing Authority sites. But we started getting requests from community groups because people were out of work, so we ended up making dinner boxes. We'd prepare a boxed dinner for four."

The initiative was supported by all Hospitality Group brands, including 15 restaurants and countless Parkhurst team members operating out of the Parkhurst location at PNC First Side. Depending on the size of the community, Brooks and his team would provide community centers with one or two deliveries every week. In some cases, United Way provided funding directly to community centers to augment meal programs already in place.

The demand was growing so quickly, Eat'n Park could no longer provide enough storage. Trusted partners Turner Dairy Farms and US Foodservice came to the rescue by making their refrigerated trucks available. For five months, refrigerated trucks were parked on the dock at PNC First Side and outside the Homestead Eat'n Park.

"As we made the meals, we put them into the trucks," Brooks says. "Whoever was making the deliveries – sometimes it was me, other times it was a school bus, other times a variety of people – would take the meals out of the truck, and off they would go."

And then there was Thanksgiving 2020. "We provided 50,000 Thanksgiving dinners. Each box had enough food to feed six people," Brooks says. "It was a traditional meal – turkey, mashed potatoes, gravy, stuffing, and vegetables."

What started as emergency support to one school district evolved into Eat'n Park's eventual distribution of more than 1.3 million meals.

Family Support

The leadership of Eat'n Park Hospitality Group was acutely aware that the pandemic was creating financial challenges for team members, too. "I knew we would need to make very painful decisions in the short term in order to come out on the other side healthy and strong and with our culture intact," Jeff reflects.

When Jeff defined the two objectives for surviving the pandemic, implicit in each was maintaining the culture of the company. The company's purpose to "Create a Smile" applies to team members, as well as the community, and Jeff and his team went to great lengths to create smiles for team members during the pandemic.

The pandemic had the potential to threaten the culture that had been nurtured over decades. "Downsizing was the heaviest moment," reflects Beth Codner, senior vice president and chief people officer. "That was a tough, tough realization – especially for those that are long-tenured leaders who have steered a very loyal and loving, caring, fun workforce for years. It wasn't a shock that we had to make the decision to downsize; it was a shock that we made it. We knew we had to, but this company hadn't any history of it."

The decision to downsize weighed heavily on Jeff.

"Jeff is extremely relaxed, he's funny, and he loves life," says Patty Shell. "But the priorities had shifted; his focus was on the long-term, and he knew that meant making very hard decisions. The day the furloughs were announced was probably the hardest day ever for him."

Jeff and his team knew that communication with team members would be more important than ever during this unprecedented period. "I made it clear that I intended to communicate with transparency the changes that we were implementing," Jeff explains. "And I encouraged my entire management team to do the same."

To ease the challenges that would result from the furloughs, the company looked for ways to provide a bridge to federal programs. "We wanted to retain team members," Trina DeMarco, director of corporate communications and community partnerships, says. "But we also knew the best way to ensure their financial security was to put them on furlough so that they could access the benefits available to them through the government."

The financial challenges created by the pandemic were so significant, the company formed the Eat'n Park Hospitality Group Foundation. Separate from the business, the foundation has its own board of directors and exists to provide small, short-term emergency grants to team members through the Team Member Assistance Fund. The fund was established through the support of the Broadhurst Family Foundation and Eat'n Park Hospitality Group.

Eat'n Park and Parkhurst also created food pantries for their team members, enabling them to choose any food that wasn't being used. "We gave our team members as much fresh food as we could," Trina says.

In addition, Eat'n Park provided restaurant team members with up to four free meals every week for the first month of the furloughs and a full meal for Thanksgiving and Christmas. The effort involved many of the company's functions, including menu development, purchasing, and communication. "We created a communication process for reaching affected team members," Trina says. "We told them dinner was on us on Tuesdays and Thursdays, pointed them to the menu, and asked them to respond so we'd know how many dinners to prepare."

Broadhurst Bingo

Jeff Broadhurst, outgoing and fun loving by nature, wanted to find a way to see his colleagues who had been distanced by COVID. The solution was virtual Broadhurst Bingo that team members joined via Zoom.

"When we can bring joy, we'll bring it in a way that resonates with this company," says Beth Codner. As a newer member of Eat'n Park Hospitality Group's leadership team, Beth witnessed the company's culture in action during the COVID pandemic. "I was really impressed by how our leaders brought joy in ways that resonated with the company."

Team members who registered received a bingo box sent to their home in advance filled with everything a bingo fanatic would crave – multiple bingo cards, dobbers, popcorn, candy, and more.

Mark and Jeff Broadhurst donned their tuxedos to carry out their bingo responsibilities.

Brothers Jeff and Mark were the self-appointed callers, and Kathy James and Patty Shell served as "bingo girls," directing participants' attention to the prizes and adding a touch of elegance with their party clothes.

Of course, Jeff and Mark couldn't simply call the numbers; they had to add their own style. After Jeff announced the bingo number, Mark used his best bingo lingo to echo the numbers called using terms like "Number 30 – Dirty Girty," "Number 83 – time for tea," and "22 – double ducks." The brothers' entertaining humor contrasted with their formal (mostly) attire.

"Mark had a special talent – he had a saying for everything," Carol Kijanka says. "And Jeff and Mark tortured each other throughout the game."

Broadhurst Bingo was a fiercely competitive activity, with prizes ranging from bottles of wine and toilet plungers to gift cards and flip-flop flyswatters.

"People loved it, and Jeff loved it," Patty remembers. "It was amazing, the excitement that he had seeing everyone on Zoom. And after that first time with the Corporate Support Center, he wanted to do it again. So, we did it with the restaurant general managers. And then he wanted to do it again, so we did it with the Parkhurst folks. It was important to him to stay connected," Patty reflects. "He will never allow there to be a separation; even though people were remote, they were still connected."

Jeff's enthusiasm was contagious.

"As senior leaders, Jeff and Mark understood very early on that if you don't let people embrace the joy in life when it's available, all you are doing then is getting consumed by the darkness – and that's not mentally healthy for anyone," Beth says.

Jeff Broadhurst's love of life brings a smile to everyone, including Patty Shell.

Zooming in on Relationships

For Parkhurst Dining, the pandemic affected both college and corporate accounts. Some corporate accounts closed entirely, while most colleges moved to remote learning, leaving a skeletal staff and few students.

"We're about people, so before the pandemic, everything we did with clients was in person," Carol Kijanka explains. But, during the pandemic, client contact initially was limited to correspondence and Zoom calls.

That just wasn't the Parkhurst way.

Jeff and Mark Broadhurst knew that clients enjoyed socializing. "They came up with an idea of a virtual event," Carol says. "It wasn't to be business related; it had to be educational and fun."

The creativity of Parkhurst leadership, combined with the logistical expertise of Carol, and the willingness of business partners gave birth to a series of events for clients conducted over Zoom. First up: a wine-tasting event.

"We have a vendor who sells Italian wines," Carol says. "So we purchased bottles of wine and paired them with foods like cheese, crackers, and sardines. I packaged everything and shipped it to clients." On the designated evening, Parkhurst leaders and clients gathered via Zoom to enjoy a wine class, learning about different varietals, best pairings, and fun facts.

The session was so well received, Jeff and Mark added virtual events that focused on other food and beverages. In one case, Mark joined famed Mexican chef Rick Bayless in Chicago for a Zoom session in which clients learned to make the famous Rick Bayless Guacamole. In advance, Parkhurst provided clients with the avocados, onions, and lemons.

Virtual events are just one example of how Parkhurst found innovative ways to keep engaged with clients while adapting operations to a rapidly changing environment. Carol concludes, "It was amazing to me how Parkhurst folks just embraced it and kept on moving."

Compassion as a Defining Value

"As a result of the pandemic, we've learned a lot about ourselves and about who we are as a team," Jeff concludes. "We've always been a company that cares, and throughout this experience, caring has been amplified – how we care for each other, our team members, our guests and clients, our community.

"Would I ever want to experience something like this again? Absolutely not," he says emphatically, "but we achieved our objectives – we took care of each other, and we emerged a stronger company with our culture intact. And we learned that 'strength' can be defined in many ways. As a result of this experience, we're a stronger team, we're stronger partners in our communities, our ability to pivot and to innovate is stronger. And those are strengths that we are building on to ensure that our company's future is successful and exciting."

11

Eat'n Park
Hospitality Group Culture
A Family of 10,000

The term "company culture" generally refers to a company's personality: how employees interact; how customers or clients are gained and retained; how the company is perceived internally and externally; what the company values.

The company culture at Eat'n Park Hospitality Group is so infused throughout the organization, it is almost palpable. Larry Hatch readied the soil for a culture of innovation, diligent work, and service. "Larry was willing to take well-calculated risks; he was comfortable carving new paths," Jim Broadhurst says. "And the results were innovative. He also valued dedication, which he demonstrated through his presence at the office every day until his death in 1998 when he was 91 years old."

Many team members credit the founder's son-in-law for planting the seeds of Eat'n Park's culture. "Mr. Moore founded the culture of service and community and believing in a better something," says Dominic Fricioni, district manager with Eat'n Park Restaurants. "He always, always, always supported his managers."

If Bob Moore planted the seeds of culture, then Jim Broadhurst nurtured them to develop a culture that has sustained the company. Having accompanied Bob on visits to the restaurants in his early years, Jim embraced Mr. Moore's style of getting to know team members, and he adapted it to create his own style.

"We care about our team members," Jim explains. "We do with them what we would do with anyone we care for. We ask about their family, send them notes if they're sick, try to enhance communications."

"It's a caring community," Suzy Broadhurst adds. "We look out for each other. We're all in it for the same reason – we all want to be successful, and we all want to be proud of where we work."

Sometimes, that team-member pride carries over into homes. "Our team members engage their family in the brand experience," says Trina DeMarco. "The whole family feels like they work for Eat'n Park. It's really cool. My kids have only known me as a mom who works for Eat'n Park. They take pride in that. They feel like they're a part of the Eat'n Park family. And that is not a unique experience here."

Dave Tomb, district manager, Eat'n Park Restaurants, remembers, "Jim Broadhurst could walk into your restaurant at 8:00 at night, and he would always make a point to walk around and talk to the cooks and the dishwashers. He'd ask them how they were and thank them for what they were doing. He would ask questions and take a little extra time back there."

"Mr. Moore and Jim were pretty similar in style, especially when it came to caring about people," adds Mike Corrigan, director of operations, Restaurant Division. "For both of them, it was about family and treating your family right, treating your employees right."

The concept of team members as family is something Basil Cox, former president of Eat'n Park Restaurants, looks back on fondly. "This enormous, 10,000-person family is Eat'n Park," he says. "It's quite remarkable that kind of thing can exist today and that everybody can feel part of a family that large."

Jeff Broadhurst continues to foster the sense of family today.

"That's the one thing that all of us take to heart – people come first. We really do care about our team members. People come here to work because they buy into our mission. Then they carry that forward in how they interact with our guests. When I see our servers, I see that our guests are their life, their family, and they treat them that way. Our team members are incredible people."

Jeff adapted the hospitality company's purpose and mantra to "Create a Smile" in 2018, tying into the company's iconic Smiley symbol. It begins with the leadership team, and team members bring it to life with a passion.

"Our purpose is to 'Create a Smile,' so we try to make sure that we keep a jovial atmosphere," Jeff explains. "We try to create a smile by treating people with respect and dignity, no matter where they come from or their role in the organization," he continues. "Treating people with respect and dignity – that's the most important thing our parents taught us."

The growth and expansion of Eat'n Park – from family restaurants to specialty restaurants to a contract dining service – did not change the company's commitment to people, to community, and to creating smiles across business units, decades, and geographies.

Eat'n Park Hospitality Group Core Values

We care about people.

We are passionate about food.

We seek innovation.

We are fiscally responsible.

We advance diversity, equity, and inclusion.

"The culture really starts with Jim and Suzy," says JoAnn Walk, district manager, Hello Bistro. "They model it. The Broadhursts and the great managers I worked with instilled the culture in me, and now I instill it in others."

When Eat'n Park Hospitality Group rolled out the core values, Karen Bolden – chief people officer at the time – was concerned. One of the values gave her pause: We are passionate about food. Of course, team members in the restaurants and Parkhurst would be passionate about food, but how could that value be infused among team members in the Corporate Support Center?

"I was a little anxious," Karen admits. "How on earth can you possibly train and develop a passion for food in places like our office?" Karen's concerns quickly abated.

"It was so cool," she remembers. "I'd hear people talking about cooking, we had a community-supported agriculture program that people signed up for so they could buy produce directly from farmers, there were wine tastings. People tried, people cared, and people developed a curiosity about food and that drove their passion. It was contagious."

Team Appreciation

Hospitality is a challenging business. According to Dan Wilson, chief financial officer, "It's a fun business, but every day, it's a hard job."

That's why Dan spearheaded the development of an annual initiative to demonstrate that the corporate leaders understand and appreciate the responsibilities team members fulfill every day.

Dan Wilson introduced Team Member Appreciation Day in 1990.

Every spring, team members from the Corporate Support Center spend a day at restaurants and contract dining locations, often trying to take on the responsibilities of team members. That might mean making a milkshake, decorating Smiley Cookies, or serving hungry college students.

"On Team Appreciation Day, we get everybody out into the field," Dan explains. "We go out and work, we see what it's like. It gives us a little appreciation for the decisions we're making."

The first Employee Appreciation Day (later called Team Member Appreciation Day) was held on May 4, 1990. Dan's idea for the day was inspired by his own experience when he joined the company as vice president of corporate planning. He told Jim Broadhurst that since he had never worked in a restaurant, he needed that experience. "It wasn't just like a day or two," Dan says with a laugh. "I worked shifts for two weeks at the Whitehall restaurant washing dishes, preparing food, and cooking."

Dan found the experience so valuable that he suggested to Jim that the company dedicate one day a year when team members from the office would leave to work in the field. "It sounded like something that would be good for the company," he says.

The idea was for office staff to experience the challenges of team members' jobs and – even more importantly – to thank them for what they do every day to fulfill the company's purpose to "Create a Smile."

When the concept was introduced at the office, it didn't do much for Dan's popularity. "It didn't go over particularly well," he remembers. "People thought they'd be disruptive and didn't see how it would be good for business."

The first year, everyone did the same thing: made strawberry pies in preparation for Mother's Day – the peak season for strawberry pies. In the early years, office staff worked the salad bar, or in the bakery, or cooked. "Some years were edgier than others," Dan says. "But as time went on, we hit every one of the departments."

What began as a dedicated day has evolved, growing as the company grew to include Parkhurst Dining, The Porch, and Hello Bistro. "We have more accounts than we have people who can cover them," Dan explains, "so now we have a two-month timeframe."

The tepid reception that office staff initially gave Dan gave way to excitement. "It's an opportunity for us to learn from team members. It's pretty eye-opening when people see how complicated the job is."

The experience also provides a different type of awareness. "Most folks come back with stories about how much of a family it is," Dan says. "You can really sense that everybody covers for each other. They are more than a bunch of friends; they're family."

"Most folks come back with stories about how much of a family it is,"

Dan says. "You can really sense that everybody covers for each other.

They are more than a bunch of friends; they're family."

Thank You for Not Smoking

Throughout its seven-decade history, Eat'n Park frequently has utilized signs to communicate important messages. From early-day window announcements about menu specials to today's outdoor LED marquees, messages for guests have always been easy to see. However, there was one sign that appeared in the lobbies of Eat'n Park restaurants that caught many by surprise.

On May 31, 2007, guests at Eat'n Park restaurants were greeted by a sign stating that the restaurants were completely smoke free. Historically, Eat'n Park restaurants had a designated smoking section, often framed by glass partitions. Now, partitions were removed, making the entire footprint of restaurants smoke free.

The decision followed a smoke-free trial at five Eat'n Park locations. Although the results of the trial were inconclusive, the company's leadership chose to move forward with the change. Jeff Broadhurst and the leadership team recognized that the smoke-free decision was going to be controversial and would have a financial impact. In addition to an estimated cost of $150,000 to clean and convert the former smoking areas, the team knew the restaurants would experience a decline in business.

"This is not a financial decision," Jeff said at the time. "It's a decision to do what is right for our team members and guests." The company went so far as to offer a year-long smoking cessation program – including one-on-one counseling – for team members.

"We have a responsibility to protect the health of our team members and guests," Jeff said. "The core of our guests will appreciate the smoke-free environment, but we also have many longtime guests who we know wish we would not make this change."

Sixteen months after Eat'n Park went smoke free, the Commonwealth of Pennsylvania's smoke-free-restaurant legislation went into effect.

"It was a difficult decision," Jeff says now. "But I absolutely would make the same decision again."

"This is not a financial decision. It's a decision to do what is right for our team members and guests."

— Jeff Broadhurst

Fielding a Team

In the restaurant industry, planning and timing are keys to success. Leave it to Eat'n Park team members to apply the same precision to softball. Yes, softball.

In the late 1970s and early 1980s, a group of managers would get together informally to socialize – see a show, take in a movie, or just enjoy each other's company over dinner, and every once in a while, they would play softball. In 1982, the group asked around to see if other team members would be interested in joining them to play softball. The response was enthusiastic.

The three restaurant managers – Don Michaels, Dennis Quinlisk, and Milt Dunsey – decided to pay a visit to Jim Broadhurst. "We asked Jim if we were permitted to form a softball league," Don explains. "Jim was all for it. He loves friendly competition, both at work and outside of work. Once he gave us the green light, we started off with three fields – Boyce Park, South Park, and West End."

Don, Dennis, and Milt did some research, formalized the plans, and created the Eat'n Park Softball League. Teams were comprised of team members from each restaurant that chose to participate. Each team was required to have at least three women. As word spread about the opportunity, additional restaurants formed teams, and Don was regarded as the softball commissioner.

It didn't take long to see that team members had two strong traits – talent and a love of competition.

Don, Dennis, and Milt put the guidelines in place: teams would be divided into four geographic regions, and the winner of each region would advance to the playoffs. The winning team would earn a trophy to be displayed in their restaurant. "It's a fun time but also very competitive because everyone wants to win the championship," Don says.

Jeff Broadhurst officially appointed Don the softball commissioner in 2007. Since then, one of Don's annual responsibilities is to meet with his committee to create a bracket for the championship playoffs. He says, "We now let everybody in the playoffs, not just the top teams for each division."

The Eat'n Park Softball League provides an opportunity for stars to shine. In fact, each season ends with an all-star game. Don explains, "We get two players from each team and form two teams. We have the North/South playing the East/West, and we have two games going on simultaneously." The all-star game draws a crowd. "It's popular because everybody wants to see who the best players are in the league."

Another highlight of every season is the legends game, often referred to as the "old-timers" game. Like every other aspect of the softball league, the criteria for being a legend is well defined. "You have to have worked for the company for at least 25 years, you have to be at least 40 years old, and you have to have two years of nonactive play," the softball commissioner says. Although the winner has bragging rights, Don explains that – more importantly – the loser has crying rights.

The legends event ends with a fiercely competitive company trivia competition, with the accuracy of answers sometimes debated.

The softball league was a bright idea, but a case of mistaken identity could have prevented it from ever taking shape.

"The day that Dennis, Milt, and I went to talk with Jim Broadhurst about forming a league, the four of us were standing around in a hallway chit-chatting about stuff," Don remembers. "Mr. Hatch, the founder, came by, and he thought the three of us were electricians. He said, 'You guys gonna fix that outlet in my office?'"

Silver Celebrations

When Eat'n Park Restaurants reached its 25th anniversary in 1974, there were a number of team members who had been with the company since the first year. By the late 1970s, the number was growing, and Jim decided people should be recognized for their loyalty. That idea became the Quarter Century Club.

The Quarter Century Club recognizes team members who have worked for any of the Eat'n Park Hospitality Group brands for 25 years. Each year, a new class of team members is inducted into the club. They are recognized at a dinner where they join the members who have already celebrated the silver milestone. The celebration is limited to only team members who have been with the company for 25 years and their guest. No exceptions.

The first class of the Quarter Century Club was comprised of four dedicated team members: Paul Baker, Dorothy Carroll, Bill McKinsey, and John Vichie. Over seven decades, the club has grown to more than 700 members.

For one member of the first class – Dorothy Carroll – the Quarter Century Club was particularly important. Dorothy, who was the administrative assistant to Larry Hatch and Bill Peters, joined the company shortly after opening day and attended the event every year – even when she was 100 years old. "She was always meticulously dressed," says Kathy James. "Every year, she would have one of her sons accompany her to the dinner. Everyone looked forward to seeing her."

Dorothy Carroll, one of the first Eat'n Park employees, annually attended Quarter Century Club dinners, even when she was 100 years old.

Dorothy, like many Quarter Century Club members, attended the annual event long after she retired. "Once you're a part of the team, you're always part of the team, even after retirement," Suzy Broadhurst explains.

"These members are special people. They're part of the reason for Eat'n Park Hospitality Group's success," Jim Broadhurst adds. "Over the years, people have come and gone, jobs have changed, responsibilities have evolved, challenges and successes have continued. But all of the Quarter Century Club members have made a positive impact on the company, and for that, we are forever grateful."

The first class of the Quarter Century Club was comprised of four dedicated team members: Paul Baker, Dorothy Carroll, Bill McKinsey, and John Vichie. Over seven decades, the club has grown to more than 700 members.

Bringing the Mission to Life

"Our team members are really proud of the company, proud of what they do. You see all these people that love working here," Mark Broadhurst notes. "There is a culture and legacy built here."

Brooks Broadhurst has no hesitation about identifying what has enabled the company culture to transcend time and place. "Dad," he says confidently. "He has been able to build a company and move it from where it was to where it is today by hiring and retaining the right people – putting the right people in the right jobs. And he always allowed people to do their jobs."

"The culture might have been built from the leadership a long time ago," Mark says, "but it's taken on a life of its own. The culture has grown with the organization of 70-plus years."

John Rusnock, a retired district manager with the Restaurant Division, notes, "The company invests in good people. Investing is not always compensation and promotion," he explains. "It's talking to good people, keeping them involved, making sure they feel they are important and have worth."

Prior to her role as district manager with Hello Bistro restaurants, JoAnn Walk held the same position with Eat'n Park. She remembers one meeting with a group of team members that included four people who were recently hired. JoAnn explains, "Part of what we do is ask, 'What can we do to make your job better? What can we do to make you happier?' The new team members were just so amazed," JoAnn says. "At the end of that meeting, they said, 'No other company does this.'"

"Our culture centers around people – team members, guests, and the community," Jeff explains. "Our purpose is 'Create a Smile.' It's simple and easy to understand and easy to remember. I mean, if we don't have people, then nothing else really matters."

The culture of innovation and dedication that Larry Hatch began, seeded by Bob Moore's focus on service and community, and nurtured by Jim Broadhurst's passion to create a family of team members, is the foundation for the company's past, present, and future success.

That culture, which begins at the company's headquarters in western Pennsylvania and extends throughout the mid-west and east, is at the heart of Eat'n Park Hospitality Group's brand of hospitality. The strength of the company's culture is the foundation on which Jeff Broadhurst and today's Hospitality Group leaders are building.

"Our core values, our purpose, our team members, our excitement about growth – that's what sets us up for success in the future," Jeff says emphatically. "And," Brooks observes, "I think the organization is stronger than it's ever been. I think the opportunities are endless."

"We'll continue to create smiles," Mark adds, "and we'll do it through food and people."

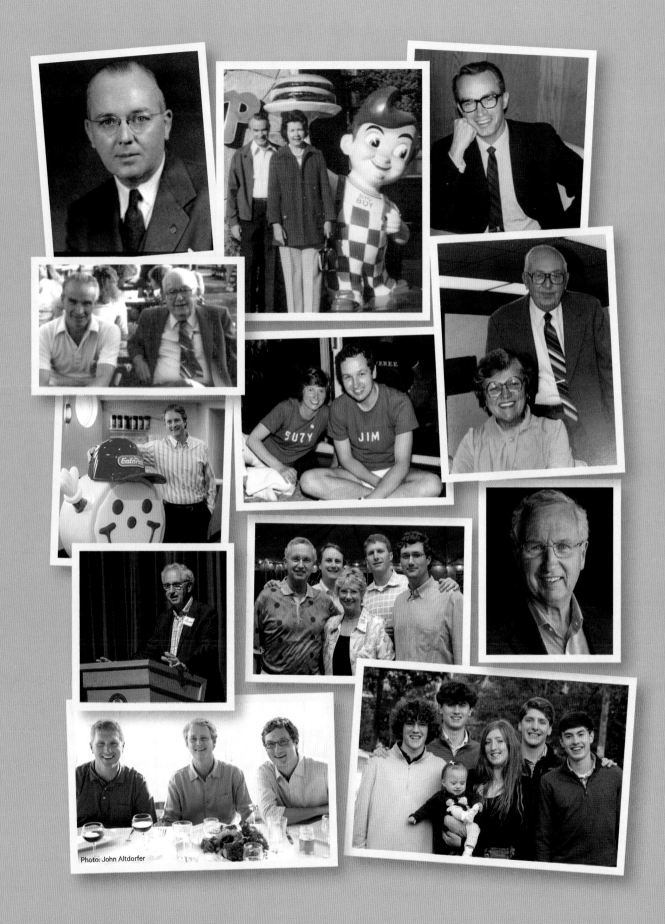

Photo: John Altdorfer

Epilogue

As the pandemic wanes and Eat'n Park Hospitality Group gradually gets back up to speed, changes remain, as do challenges. As I look back at the impact the pandemic has had, I realize that an experience I had as a young man helped the company weather the storm.

My grandfather was an Episcopal minister at a small church in Titusville, Pennsylvania. He died when I was a teenager, and shortly after his death, my father asked me to help clear out my grandfather's attic. There were many other things I would have preferred to do other than cleaning out an attic.

My grandfather had accumulated a number of boxes and chests. As we rummaged through years of dust and dirt, my father told me that if I saw anything I wanted, I could have it. I really wanted something of importance to my grandfather, who I loved very much, but I couldn't imagine that there was anything in that musty old attic that would pique my interest.

But after a short time, I noticed a small blackboard in the corner of the attic. Painted in fading letters on that blackboard was the message: "There is no limit to the good you can do if you don't care who gets the credit."

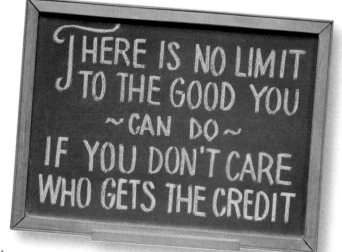

When I uncovered that blackboard, I also uncovered the essence of my grandfather's life. The blackboard was a small item to take from my grandfather's attic that day, but it has had a huge effect on me. And I have made my grandfather's message, which hangs in the office today, the guiding philosophy of my life and a guiding principle in the culture of Eat'n Park.

Over the course of my 50-year involvement with Eat'n Park, I've witnessed how working together as a team can bring everyone together for the greater good. One team that consistently demonstrates that is our company's Board of Directors.

Although our board has grown in size and complexity in parallel with the evolution of our company, their dedication has remained steadfast. Today's board members have been encouraging and enthusiastic when we have pursued opportunities, like expansion of our brands or geography; and they have been a source of counsel and support through challenges, like weathering the storm of the pandemic. I am grateful for their countless contributions to our success.

On a daily basis, our team members also embody my grandfather's message – working together for the greater good. Their dedication to our guests, clients, and each other is gratifying, and their support of our communities is inspiring.

As Suzy and I share *The Story Behind the Smile*, we do so with great pride in our sons and the team they have built to carry on the business and traditions of Eat'n Park Hospitality Group.

Eat'n Park Hospitality Group 2022 Board of Directors. (left to right:) Dan Wilson, Brooks Broadhurst, Christy Uffelman, Mark Broadhurst, Toni Murphy, John Surma, Chuck Cohen, Jim Broadhurst, Suzy Broadhurst, Jeff Brown, and Jeff Broadhurst

Acknowledgements

Writing *The Story Behind the Smile* was the greatest honor of my career. I offer my profound gratitude to Suzy and Jim Broadhurst and the Broadhurst family for entrusting me to tell the story of Eat'n Park Hospitality Group. Their generosity of time, spirit, and support inspired me throughout the process of researching, writing, and editing this book.

The book is possible only because of the cooperation and assistance of so many people. I interviewed more than 60 people, some of whom are mentioned in the book, and some of whom provided equally valuable information for background. I am indebted to each of them.

I thank my initial editors, Patricia McMahon, PhD, and Sue Cardillo, whose input ensured the content was not only grammatically correct, but also relayed information in an understandable and interesting manner. And I thank Caitie Fink, an extraordinary grammarian, and Carol Kijanka for their excellent proofreading skills.

The initial cover concept for *The Story Behind the Smile* was developed by Scot Wallace of Scot Wallace Design. The stories were brought to life by Mike Vogel and John Rossey from MJ Creative Team. Many people contributed photography, and most current-day photos were from the lens of Adam Stephenson. I am grateful to each for their vision and creativity.

The Story Behind the Smile would not have been possible without Kathy James. I forever will be grateful for and indebted to her. The owner of institutional history, Kathy provided invaluable insight, guidance, and details throughout every stage of the process. Her knowledge of the company, the culture, and the individuals helped to shape the content of the book. With each word, sentence, chapter, and draft, Kathy always was an absolute delight to work with. She was – and is – an indispensable collaborator and friend.

Writing this book has taught me that Eat'n Park Hospitality Group team members live the company's purpose to "Create a Smile." Without a doubt, theirs are the stories behind the smile.

About the Author

Lynn McMahon is an award-winning writer and public relations practitioner living in Pittsburgh. Over the course of her career, she has worked with iconic companies and organizations in Pittsburgh and across the country. Her flair for storytelling as well as her talent for communicating with precision and depth have made her a sought-after writer and ghost writer. She has developed content for magazines, editorials, speeches, newsletters, and websites. Lynn is also a highly valued crisis communication consultant whose skills are often in demand, perhaps more than ever during the pandemic.

From her earliest days as vice president of public relations at Children's Hospital of Pittsburgh when organ transplantation was in its infancy to co-owning her own public relations agency to her current position as an agency vice president of public relations, Lynn has been an integral part of Pittsburgh's communication community, a steward of her profession, bringing her sense of integrity to each job and each role of her impressive career.

Lynn holds a Bachelor of Arts degree in writing from the University of Pittsburgh and a Master of Arts degree in corporate communication from Duquesne University.

Everyone who grew up with Eat'n Park has stories to tell and, for Lynn, it's been a privilege to share them through *The Story Behind the Smile*. She can be reached at PenAndPaper412@gmail.com.

Bibliography

Batz Jr., Bob. "So, You Ask, Just Who Are the Stars behind Eat'n Park's Christmas Tree Commercial?" *Pittsburgh Post-Gazette* (December 5, 2018). https://www.post-gazette.com/ae/2018/12/05/Eat-N-Park-Christmas-star-tree-special-lift-TV-commercial-holiday-Pittsburgh/stories/201811280144?cid=search

Butko, Brian. *Klondikes, Chipped Ham, & Skyscraper Cones: The Story of Isaly's.* Pittsburgh, Stackpole Books, First Edition, 2001.

Lait, Matt. "Bob Wian, Founder of Bob's Big Boy Dies at 77." Los Angeles Times (April 1, 1992).

Moore, Bob. *Welcome to Eat'n Park, The Early Days.* June 2002

Nichols, Chris. "This Vintage Bob's Big Boy Film Is a 1940s-Era Treasure." *LAMag.com:* https://www.lamag.com/askchris/vintage-bobs-big-boy-training-film-1940s-era-treasure/.

Roddey, Dennis B. "Obituary: William D. Peters/President of Eat'n Park Restaurants." *Pittsburgh Post-Gazette* (August 20, 2000).

"Balloons Over Iowa Newsletter." https://www.balloons-over-Iowa club.com/PDFs/TnG45Sept06.pdf. September - October 2006.

"The Beginning of an Icon." https://www.BigBoy.com. https://www.latimes.com/archives/la-xpm-1992-04-01-me-242-story.html

"Forgotten Los Angeles." Facebook.com: https://www.facebook.com/ForgottenMadnessLA/posts/bobs-pantry-in-glendale-est-1936-home-of-the-big-boy-burgersyes-thats-right-85-y/233158842248306/.

"Frisch's Brawny Lad and Big Boy Mascots." https://dannwoellertthefoodetymologist.wordpress.com/2017/03/19/frischs-brawny-lad-and-big-boy-mascots/.

"Guide to the Eat'n Park Photographs, 1958-1998." HistoricPittsburgh.com: https://historicpittsburgh.org/islandora/object/pitt%3AUS-QQS-msp491/viewer. Hosted by the University of Pittsburgh Library System. Repository: Heinz History Center.

"The Untold Truth of Big Boy." https://www.mashed.com/176193/the-untold-truth-of-big-boy.